Conversations
with Uncle O. R. Tambo

To David
Many thanks for your
support and solidarity!
Lindiwe Mabuza
18/6/19

Conversations
with Uncle O. R. Tambo

CHILDHOOD MEMOIRS IN EXILE

Edited by Lindiwe Mabuza

REAL AFRICAN PUBLISHERS

Published by Real African Publishers
PO Box 3317
Houghton 2041
Johannesburg

MEMORY IS *our*
heritage

www.mutloatse.com.

© individual authors

ISBN: 978-1-928341-02-4

Editor:	Lindiwe Mabuza
Project manager:	Mothobi Mutloatse
Production editor:	Reedwaan Vally
Text editor:	Angela McClelland
Book design:	Adam Rumball

Published December 2017

arts & culture
Department:
Arts and Culture
REPUBLIC OF SOUTH AFRICA

Real African Publishers and Mothobi Mutloatse (Memory Is Our Heritage) wish to thank the Department of Culture for underwriting the publication of this unique childhood memoir; all of the contributors, including the editor, Ambassador Lindiwe Mabuza; Minister Nathi Mthethwa, Acting Deputy Director General (Arts); Lisa Combrinck, and Sithembiso Ntombela; and the editorial and production team led by publisher Reedwaan Vally, Angela McClelland, Adam Rumball, Nthabiseng Mhlongo and Matthew Nkosi.

All photographs of SOMAFCO, unless indicated otherwise, are by David Max Brown, and individual portraits were loaned from their private collections. The publisher undertakes to correct any omission or commission if so directed by any person, in a future reprint.

Life and legacy of OR TAMBO. 100 YEARS

CONTENTS

INTRODUCTION
Born of his love of culture, the arts, music and the written word

When I tell friends about this book, they express amazement. But where and how did the notion come about? The answer is simple. The genesis of this book resides deep in the DNA of Oliver Tambo's ANC: his ethical, principled, visionary, humane and compassionate practical leadership. It is born of his love of culture, the arts in general, music, and the written word, in particular.

All of us who had the special 'once-in-a-lifetime' privilege of being led, taught, counselled, admonished and guided by President Oliver Reginald Tambo in the global struggle to liberate our country will forever be indebted to him for all of the lessons he constantly and generously gave. Not a braggart, his humility and selflessness conquered many a heart.

Oliver Tambo helped pull many of us with our flat-footedness of soul to run the race with him. So when 2017 was declared the centenary year of his birthday, we asked ourselves how we might, in a meaningful way, honour him and enable our people to know and appreciate the scope of the huge work he accomplished. As President Thabo Mbeki says, 'Oliver Reginald Tambo is the father of our democracy.'

For the 90th anniversary of his birthday, with Mrs Adelaide Tambo's encouragement, we initiated and compiled contributions from around 80 people from various countries and from different walks of life in a volume edited by Pallo Jordan and published by Pan Macmillan titled *Oliver Tambo Remembered*. The contributors were Comrades in the alliance he worked closely with, heads of state, dignitaries, journalists, business people, artists, etc.

For the 100th anniversary of his birth, we thought we would approach those who were children under his watch. I ran the idea past two dynamic young ladies of The Melting Pot: Gcina Mdlulwa and Mandlakazi Mpumlwana, who found their niche in O. R.'s passion for choral music.

Those two young ladies inspired me hugely. Since 2013, they have been training conductors, holding popular national competitions and festivals, and commissioning special compositions about O. R. With the encouragement of such O. R. enthusiasts and a draft in hand addressed to Masupatsela a Walter Sisulu (Pioneers), the process started.

I was quite excited when my niece, Pulane Kingston, agreed to be the intermediary between the prospective writers and me. She has been extraordinary and most vigilant in carrying that out, often under pressure. Many of the responses brought tears to my eyes, and the high quality of all of the letters is already making O. R. smile his typical victory smile.

There is so much such love, enthusiasm and gratitude for and to 'Uncle'! The palpable nostalgia for his leadership easily fills the pages. I got a sense, with almost all of the letters, that the act of opening oneself to the most trusted father-confessor was akin to a therapy session. Perhaps the fact that I was known as 'Aunty Lindi' to almost all of them couldn't have hurt the process, either.

Why Aunty? In exile, we maintained much that is positive in our African culture. All grown-ups were aunties and uncles, and all children were ours together. We were our brothers' and sisters' keepers, so to speak. In Lusaka, where my interaction with many of our authors started, we were a vibrant, closely knit ANC community where mutual interdependence was a norm.

Together, young and old, we would gather to mark important events in our history: 8 January, 8 March, 16 June, 9 August, 16 December, which, respectively, are: the founding of the ANC, International Women's Day, the Soweto Uprising (now Youth Day), South African Women's Day, and the founding of MK. Each one of those events was an opportunity to learn from the leadership and from each other. We would also participate in the events of other liberation movements.

All of our children attended either a local or an international school, where the standard of education was far superior to Bantu

Children: Sisonke Msimang and Thandiwe Modise
Adults: Lindiwe Mabuza and Jackie Modise

Education. Apart from hating apartheid, some parents, like the Gaobepes, had chosen to leave South Africa in order to ensure quality education for their children. Over weekends, our children attended extra classes led by Mrs Rita Mfenyana and Ms Ntombi Cheela.

Those would include the history of South Africa, Africa, the ANC, and International Solidarity as Mrs Zanele Mbeki explains in the Foreword. Every weekend, groups of children of varying ages (named the Masupatsela or Pioneers) would gather at Mrs Mfenyana's house for classes. The photo on the cover and some colourful pieces of art in the book are examples of the work of the Saturday school. Strong bonds were formed that endure to this day.

Practically every child who came out of Masupatsela training could sing the clauses of the Freedom Charter, the policy document of the ANC. Freedom songs were communal property, hence our children could sing them with the same eloquence and fluency they had for Chinyanja, IsiSwati or KiSwahili. That, of course, in the hands of a few precocious ones, could have curious, delightful or amusing consequences.

When the family of Mavuso Msimang left Lusaka for a new job in Nairobi, Kenya, there was no Masupatsela school for young Sisonke. In her regular class at an international school, the teacher asked all pupils to present a traditional song from their country. Of course, Sisonke knew several from her Lusaka days. When her turn came, she got up, faced the class with confidence and belted out *Sizobadubula ngembayimbayi! Bazobaleka! Dubula ngembayimbayi*! (With our machine guns, we will chase them away!)

Poor child, what chance or choice did she have? – All of them, for that matter? She had come back from school in Lusaka happily singing 'Baa baa black sheep' at age five! The subsequent talk or lecture or reprimand set her forever on the path of loving more of her country's traditional songs.

Traditional songs aside, the chances of our children being highly motivated were immeasurably greater far from the toxic environment of apartheid. By the time they completed high school, many would have had a chance to travel to one or two countries as participants in programmes that were tailor-made for children and would have added to their education immensely. Invitations for short-term visits or summer camp exposure came from a number of civic organisations in some of the socialist countries.

When 1979 was declared the International Year of the Child by the United Nations, 10 ANC children and two adults arrived in Oslo for a two-week holiday as guests of *Norsk Folksjhelp* (Norwegian People's Help). Our friends in the international community did those good deeds because they knew that their interventions would lessen the pain and bring some semblance of normalcy to those who were unable to return home to South Africa.

That was also the year that Comrade Rita Mfenyana decided that the Masupatsela children should paint, write poems and short anecdotes, and make drawings in order to produce an ANC Children's Calender. All of the ANC offices worldwide got boxes for distribution to our supporters. The women's wing of Sweden's Social Democratic Party purchased a vehicle for the ANC Women's Section so that they could transport children to their Saturday activities and for other child-related work. Constant financial and material assistance came from socialist countries as well as India, the UK, Italy, and organisations such as Unicef. Some of our authors produced material that, under normal circumstances, would have won them prizes. In my humble view, that calendar could easily have been a collector's item besides being in the ANC archives!

A few of the contributors provided vivid vignettes of their Uncle O. R. In one of them, one can actually see the awe-struck Sonja de Bruin timidly directing O. R. to the bathroom to wash his hands in her home, her heart pumping faster and faster! Deliciously ecstatic! She has seen him, so very close! Can't we imagine how a little girl feels? Put yourself in her shoes. Almost three decades later, her love and emotions for her two heroes by her bedside, Uncle and Daddy, delightfully spoiling her with their larger-than-life presence, surfaces once again ... especially precious because they aren't around anymore.

At a concert at the Solomon Mahlangu Freedom College (Somafco), Pulane Kingston so powerfully dramatises her poem against P. W. Botha that it earns her a standing ovation from a president who decides to indulge that little winner by walking around with her holding her hand. She was on Cloud Nine!

And then comes Thandiwe Modise! She forgot all about her game outside with friends as soon as she saw Uncle's car driving towards her home, for everyone must know that she saw him first! Around the same time, at Somafco, Zola Maseko, the head of Masupatsela, had a serious attack:

... as butterflies played havoc with my stomach ...

but he quickly recovered to record his first impression of the president:

What a gentle and dignified man.

Here was Nelson Mandela's friend and Comrade. Here was the man who represented the link between our leaders on Robben Island and the exiled ANC leadership. He was the link between the ANC and the international community ... he was the glue that held the ANC together throughout its most arduous years.

As the leader, Zola had the awesome task of decorating the Commander-in-Chief of uMkhonto we Sizwe with a Pioneer scarf, as required by tradition.

All of that might sound like fairyland stuff: a make-believe world where dreams turn into reality and fantasy takes children into all kinds of enticing possibilities, which, like a falling star, then quickly disappear. Surely all are entitled, at least once in a lifetime, particularly those dealt such a rotten deal by apartheid, to experience as a child the wholesome exuberance induced by someone of unfading radiance such as President O. R. Tambo.

When O. R. visited our school, there was always a state of pandemonium. Our photographer, David Brown, noted that 'even little children knew his name and sang songs in his honour'. That is not hero worship. O. R. never sought any privileges. He never denied children the right to delight when he was around.

There is a sense that O. R. genuinely had a great time with children. He also had an uncanny gift of bringing out the child in adults when relaxing with Comrades. In an interview I did with Sis Adelaide, she told of how excited their children would be whenever he came home to them in London. The only problem was that, as soon as he entered the house, Comrades would line up to see him, and consequently, the children would go to bed without seeing their father. When Sis Adelaide raised that with one Comrade, her response was 'But Comrade Adelaide, he is my father too. We need to see him as well'. O. R., who was deprived a normal family life because of the struggle, had to have the magnanimity to truly love us all, but especially the children.

One time, when I raised the question of long separations from his family, he reflected a little and then taught me this lesson. And I paraphrase:

The Comrades on Robben Island did not choose to be there. Apartheid did. Thabo Mbeki and Max Sisulu, from young ages, couldn't enjoy normal home lives and had to leave home and are here with us. Apartheid forced unnatural or abnormal decisions on children: something not in the normal order of things. Now, the ANC is their choice. The thousands of teenagers in our school in Tanzania and at our military training facilities didn't prefer to abandon parents, siblings and friends out of sheer volution or will. Apartheid forced difficult decisions on Black children. What should our answer be? Mgwenya gave the answer. MK does. I too must choose to leave those dearest to me. The Albertinas and the Winnies never choose to be thrown in prison. It all happens at apartheid's whim.

Children in exile had to grow up faster than normal to keep up with the pace at which things developed around them: school, on the one hand, and political activities, on the other. In London, Jackie and her siblings along with David Brown and Stuart Round were children engaging alongside adults in the serious work of mobilising UK citizens against apartheid. As long as you could walk, you were ready for an anti-apartheid march or demonstration. Many ANC students, such as former Governor of the Reserve Bank, Tito Mboweni and former Chairperson of the African Union, Dr Nkosazana Dlamini-Zuma, Sipho Pityana, CEO of AngloGold Ashanti not only qualified academically, their political teeth were cut on the streets of Sheffield, London, Liverpool, etc.

Going even further back in time, during the Rivonia trial, as a student, Thabo Mbeki led fellow students from Sussex University, merged with many in London, and then marched to Number 10 Downing Street to petition the Labour government of Harold Wilson to use its good offices to demand a stay of execution on the ANC/MK leadership being tried for high treason in Pretoria.

Practically the same scene repeated itself in the United States of America. When I served there as Chief Representative (Ambassador) of the ANC from 1989–1994, I had the fortune of witnessing the growth and development of some former Masupatselas: Lindiwe Sangweni and Sisonke Msimang excelled at Penn State University and McAllister College as ambassadors of our people.

I know that because, at different times, I addressed large numbers of students and faculty at arrangements they spearheaded in Pennsylvania and Minnesota.

I have no doubt that Ndlela Nkobi, Pola Mabizela, Thandiwe Njobe, Oyama Mabandla, and many others were in great demand as speakers against apartheid while they all worked so hard to maintain high grades in their studies. As students, apart from their school syllabus, they had to constantly study and update their information on events at home by monitoring the news media.

It was edifying to see that the investment made by our ANC Comrades under the leadership of President Tambo was reaping huge political dividends in terms of the mandate O. R. had been given by the ANC in 1958 of winning the world against apartheid, referred appropriately by the United Nations as 'a crime against humanity'.

Ultimately, that means that President Tambo, through the systems he put in place and through his integrity, humility, selflessness and exemplary lifestyle, was able to multiply himself – many times over – into a new generation of student fighters. We can say that he and his NEC colleagues succeeded exceedingly well in their mammoth task of rebuilding the African National Congress from outside of South Africa and mobilising the international community to deliver the final blows against apartheid. Inside South Africa, he was meticulously overseeing the resurrection of the ANC, step by step.

As a consequence of the Soweto uprising, the movement was faced with large numbers of young people who escaped the onslaught of the apartheid henchmen. Some wouldn't compromise on getting military training but, because of their age, had to be persuaded to complete high school. Normally, we would have had to send small groups to countries around the world to be educated, but the numbers dictated a different solution. A school had to be built. It was imperative.

In 1962, Tanzania was about to face a health crisis. The nurses from the UK who had been part of UK government assistance to a newly independent Tanzania were to be retracted without replacement. President Tambo persuaded the ANC in South Africa to dispatch 21 qualified nurses to Tanzania. So later, when the ANC needed to build a school, President Nyerere gave them a disused former sisal farm. (To be fair, Tanzania provided land to all liberation movements from southern Africa).

Chief Representatives of the ANC in different countries ensured the construction of the Solomon Mahlangu Freedom College (Somafco) by soliciting funding from their countries of representation, government, development aid agencies, and the public.

Our Education Committee was transformed into the Education Council, and ANC members who were teaching in some of the Frontline States were invited to Lusaka and Dar es Salaam with their curriculum proposals in their fields of expertise.

Comrade Sindiso had earlier invited an ANC member from London who had been responsible for an educational institution to join the Council, and later, Mohammed Tikly became the first principal of which, at the beginning, was a scattered collection of rundown buildings. Spencer Hodgson, an architect trained in Germany, made the architectural designs of Somafco, and later, of Dakawa. Those Comrades were joined by Oswald Dennis, the manager; and Wintshi Njobe, former head of an agricultural college in Zambia, became the next principal, while Mohammed Tikly stayed on as the chief administrator.

From its humble beginning on that former sisal farm, Somafco mushroomed into an award-winning development enterprise. We had blueprints from which prospective donors could pick and choose the item or building for which they would fundraise. Those brains in the ANC designed a crèche, primary school and secondary school with dormitories, a science block, a fully furnished hospital, a library, a teachers' block, proper homes for the teachers, and more. All of the shelves and furniture: cupboards, desks, etc. were manufactured on site. Surplus was sold at the market. Donors were in awe when Somafco created the Vuyisile Mini factory for making furniture.

Our farm had a variety of agricultural produce for the community, including a piggery, fowl runs, dairy cows and vegetables! Any surplus was sold at the local market. High-level education was guaranteed by qualified ANC teachers and volunteers from places such as the Caribbean, Scandinavia, and Europe (East and West), and Somafco was accredited by the Tanzanian Qualifications Board.

The vision of O. R. and the ANC still overwhelms one. Because of the impressive success of Somafco, the Tanzanian government gave the ANC another, even larger, settlement area called Dakawa, which became another success story!

The last principal, Ambassador Tim Maseko, oversaw the closure of Somafco and the handover of the properties to the Tanzanian government. President Nyerere decided that Somafco should become an agricultural university, which underscored the high-quality infrastructure our school had.

I spent a lot of time at the Somafco and Dakawa properties. My positive appraisal of these is not based on hearsay. When Oliver Tambo, on behalf of the ANC, handed them over to the people and government of Tanzania, Tor Sellstrom of the Swedish International Development Agency (SIDA) commented that they were 'marvels comparable to a Swedish suburb'. There they stood, monuments of the wisdom, excellence and political acumen of O. R. Tambo and his propensity to always reach beyond the skies.

But O. R. was also a very regular person: unassuming, despite being as well respected as he was. Nomsa Gaobepe tells of their especially warm, almost 'domesticated' uncle who got into their Lusaka kitchen one Christmas and roasted turkey and potatoes for their family. As he prefered, without expecting to be served, he would simply make his own tea.

Nomsa exudes love and almost childlike awe when she talks to her Uncle O. R. in her letter. Through the eyes of his nieces and nephews, we discover a man who is compassionate, even when in difficulty himself. After being struck by a stroke, O. R. walked the long hospital corridors to visit an old friend, Mary Gaobepe, who had had a third heart bypass. Intensely loyal to those who have been loyal to the ANC, he could not forget the work that Mary did going in and out of South Africa carrying messages from Lusaka to members in the underground structures of the movement.

Only O. R. is the custodian of the most critical secrets and forever shows his gratitude and indebtedness to everyone for the roles they have played on the long and hazardous road to our freedom and democracy.

President Oliver Tambo was truly our treasury of compassion. I have yet to find an ANC comrade who, if in dire straits when their path crossed his, wasn't assisted by him. O. R. would always sort out a Comrade's problem, no matter how big or small. From his example, we learned that leadership is about solving people's problems: that is where compassion comes in.

There was Bheki Langa in Russia, Thandiwe Njobe in Lusaka – both had brothers in MK. Someone had to let those two Comrades know of the manner in which their brothers died – a very tough task for any messenger. But how much more comforting and consoling when the messenger is the Commander-in-Chief, President Tambo himself, come to bring news and to help assuage the deep pain. He did not preach Ubuntu. He acted it. He lived and demonstrated it. He was their father and took upon himself the responsibility to anticipate the depth of the anguish and go down to minister, the priest that he also was, spiritually. He was fulfilling his role in his greater calling as a Moses to lead us out of the hell of apartheid. In the words of Dumisani Sangweni:

Your selflessness as a leader is surely missed today. You left our country with a suitcase and the clothes on your back, with no resources or infrastructure, and with nothing but the sheer resolve, discipline and determination, you held the ANC within your leadership team and shaped it into a formidable force outside of South Africa. Your superior interpersonal and relationship-building abilities and your ability to engage and connect is testament to how you built and shaped the ANC.

From your exemplary behaviour, you move people to emulate you and work tirelessly, mastering courage and resilience.

You are one of a kind.
A Messiah.
A towering giant.

Lindiwe Mabuza
Editor

FOREWORD
He was simply one of the most humane human beings

I am most grateful for the opportunity to accompany our children in this novel collection of letters to their 'Uncle O. R.', as Oliver Reginald Tambo, President of the African National Congress, was popularly known to the children. Undoubtedly, our understanding of 'Chief' (as he was also called by his Comrades) will be all the more enhanced as these individuals sketch their pieces in the multifaceted mosaic that our President truly was.

Today, we can correctly describe O. R. as a gentle giant. Yet, in reality, this humble, almost self-effacing, modest and very brilliant person was never larger than life. We can as well extol his extraordinary feats of leadership (and they are amazing); we can declare that his political achievement is unparalleled in the context of South African history; we can even rightly and proudly be awed by his impact on the global stage. Yet, the greatness of that phenomenal leader resides in the fact that he was the most ordinary of human beings.

Who better than his many children and grandchildren to help us discover a president many adults did not see?! Our concepts of love, understanding and compassion might be glib or even shallow at times. In these pages, we are indeed privileged to peep into private, sacred moments when his children, as they were then, lay bare their hearts, minds and souls in conversation with one held in the highest esteem: the depth and purity of their fondness, gratitude, and honest love runs throughout these pages. Inevitably today, nostalgia for his leadership haunts more than one author.

My special joy is that I have known and personally interacted with the majority of the writers in different countries as children, some even from infancy. Wherever the vicious and vile winds of apartheid scattered families, we met in Zambia, Botswana, Tanzania, Nigeria, Senegal, Lesotho, the USSR, the United Kingdom, etc.

As individuals and as families, we arrived at different points of our exile destinations and there discovered our South African-ness, our passion for justice and insatiable hunger for freedom. As members of the African National Congress, we bonded into one huge family under O. R.'s embracing leadership and committed to the values and principles of the Freedom Charter.

For any and all South Africans, whatever their political affiliation, exile was never 'a bed of roses', as the cliché goes. It had enormous challenges: physical, social, economic and psychological. After the 1976 School Pupils' Uprising, untold trauma was visited upon our youth: the trauma of forced separation, living with and amongst strangers; homesickness, loneliness, loss of the familiar; loss of frame of reference; confronting much that was foreign: land, food, language, culture, etc.

Talking of his early days in Dar es Salaam, O. R. said: 'We did not know where our next meal was coming from' (*Oliver Tambo Remembered*, edited by Pallo Jordan). Thami Ntenteni, one of the contributors to this anthology, in bold relief reminds us of how to see O. R.'s contribution thus:

Often when we remember or eulogise O. R. Tambo as a leader who possessed exceptional qualities, it is often overlooked and possibly not even considered that his feat of triumph was achieved under conditions of exile where the glorious or even triumphant episodes in an exile's life amount to no more than an effort meant to overcome the crippling sorrow of estrangement ... the loss of something left behind forever. (Reflections of Exile and other Literary and Cultural Essays by W. Edward Said)

Without exception, and to different degrees of intensity, these children, and especially their parents, also experienced estrangement. Family members hospitalised back home!

Imprisonment of a loved one! Can't return to bury a parent, a sibling or a loved one!

But these parents had to raise their children in as normal a fashion as was humanly possible under abnormal circumstances. They had to count on each other for the upbringing of the children. Since most fathers were fulltime operatives of the movement, the major role of childrearing and upkeep fell squarely and, often solely, on the shoulders of the mothers and comrades.

Those mothers, ANC activists in their own right, performed roles far beyond their family confines. They kept an open-door policy towards scores of young people coming into exile, especially after 1976: pre-eminently welding the community together by keeping some kind of social fabric and a safety net in exile! They made it possible for the menfolk to fully engage in the imperatives of the political, military and administr ative work mandated by the exigencies of the struggle. One of O. R.'s defining attributes was his ability to recognise and uphold whatever work women engaged in as valid and a significant contribution to the total liberation of our country.

The delightful fact that today we could have the sons and daughters of some of those mothers write such moving tributes

in honour of President O. R. Tambo is in large measure due to the energy, diligence, compassion, love and nurturing spirits of people like Mrs Yolisa Modise, Ambassador Thandi Rankoe-Lujabe, Mrs Sophie de Bruyn, Mrs Gertrude Shope, Mrs Angela Sangweni, Mrs Catherine Jele, Mrs Tikilili Mabizela, Mrs Adelaide Ntuli, Mrs Koleka Mabandla, Mrs Agnes Msimang, Mrs Sibanda-Tembe, and ladies who have passed on: Mrs Shope-Kubayi, MP, Mrs Tiny Nokwe, Ms Poppy Nokwe, Mrs Makho Njobe, Mrs Nompithi Maseko, Mrs Rose Motsepe, Mrs Putuse Appolus, Mrs Mary Gaobepe, Mrs 'Mangwane' Nkobi, Mrs Brown and Ms Khosi Msimang, to name but a few!

Those of us who spent some of our years in Lusaka, Zambia will never forget the tireless work and energy exerted in the political education of our children by Mrs Rita Mfenyana and Ms Ntombi Cheela. Every weekend, groups of children of varying age levels named Masupatsela would gather at her house for classes. Those would include the history of South Africa, Africa, the ANC and international solidarity. Various leaders of the ANC would take turns in helping with those classes: hence, the picture (children and O. R.) on the front cover of this book. Classes also included art and poetry.

Our school, Solomon Mahlangu Freedom College (Somafco) – built through contributions from the international community – served around 5,000 people. Credit is also due to our South African teachers as well as members of the international brigades who chose to come to Morogoro, a remote part of Tanzania, to teach subjects that were not available to Black Africans in Apartheid South Africa!

It is my wish that this book be a valuable contribution to all of the libraries of South Africa and beyond. And I also fervently hope that President Oliver Reginald Tambo, as seen through the eyes of some of his most successful protégés, will inspire millions with his impeccable leadership qualities, as he was one of the most humane human beings.

Mrs Zanele Mbeki
Former First Lady

MY EARLY DAYS WITH O. R. TAMBO

To be able to study at the respected Fort Hare University rather than go to Ongoye University, which had been established for ethnic Zulus under the grand apartheid design, I enrolled for a pharmacy degree instead of the straight BSc I had intended to study. Soon I was approached by the underground leadership of the ANC and invited to serve on the university's high command structure.

Before long, Fort Hare was being converted into a fully-fledged Bantustan university with Kaizer Matanzima appointed as chancellor. When it was announced that he would visit the university in the early part of 1963, the reaction of the students was swift and unmistakable. The boycott of the visit was so effective that only a handful of students turned up at the meeting hall for his address.

The Special Branch police were immediately set on the trail of the organisers of the boycott: I being one of the so-called ringleaders. The decision of our Port Elizabeth regional leadership was that six of us should leave the country to study abroad before the police could move in to arrest us.

After a brief stay in Johannesburg, we were on our way to Botswana and on to Dar es Salaam in Tanzania. With the arrest of the top leadership of the ANC in Rivonia on 11 July 1963, I decided that I would postpone my studies and go for military training instead. The leadership in exile welcomed that and, before long, I, along with 22 others, was on my way to Moscow. A week or so before our departure, President O. R. Tambo, accompanied by Johnny Makhathini (the longest-serving International Secretary of the ANC), paid us a visit at the Mandela residence.

A nondescript two-row guard of honour comprised of no more than 15 people was mounted for inspection by the two distinguished visitors. When he came to where I was standing, Comrade O. R. Tambo stopped, lifted his gaze to take in my height, and said: 'I'm under a tree here, a protective tree!' He beamed, his bespectacled face exposing a set of strong white teeth with prominent incisors. Years later, I would become familiar with that instant, charming and disarming smile.

In September 1964, 43 of us, fully trained in urban guerrilla warfare in Moscow, arrived in Kongwa, in the Dodoma district in Central Tanzania, to set up a transit camp alongside other liberation movements: Frelimo of Mozambique, Swapo of Namibia, and MPLA of Angola.

In 1965, after the arrival of more cadres who had received their training in Odessa, then part of the Soviet Union, and in China, Comrade O. R. made a couple of lightning visits to the camp to meet and address the guerrillas. Morale was high and a stern President Tambo addressed us. While assuring us about the certainty of our victory, he was nevertheless candid about the enormous challenges that lay ahead:

> There should be no fear in our hearts, Comrades, for we are fighting a just cause. But we should never underestimate the strength and determination of the enemy!

As he said that, the cadres listened attentively, standing in military formation.

The first significant encounter I had with the great man took place in a house in Livingstone, Zambia in 1967. It was a tense affair. He had been briefed prior to his arrival about the plan to launch a major military incursion into Rhodesia. A decision had been taken for Umkhonto weSizwe (MK) guerrillas to form a military alliance with the Zimbabwe Peoples' Revolutionary Army (Zipra), the armed wing of the Zimbabwe African Peoples' Union (Zapu). A small number of us were not convinced about the chances of success of the impending operation, mainly because

of the large number of cadres involved (about 80), the guerrillas' unfamiliarity with the area, and the sheer logistics for those earmarked to travel straight to South Africa. He asked me to suggest an alternative, and I couldn't, save to say: smaller groups, more reconnaissance and better intelligence gathering.

The fact of the matter is that all the proposals I made were already in operation and progress had been very slow. In the meantime, frustration levels in the camps had peaked and people were deserting, some to join the enemy in South Africa after traveling through Nairobi, Kenya, while others went in search of other, non-struggle-related pursuits.

There was general agitation, including within the Organisation of African Unity, about poor progress in the struggle for liberation in South Africa. For its part, the apartheid regime was mounting military and economic pressure on the Frontline States not to allow MK cadres into their countries.

It bears noting that the exigencies of the liberation wars that were being waged in southern Africa at the time favoured the establishment of the Zapu/ANC alliance. In Zimbabwe, then called Rhodesia, Zapu had started its armed struggle for liberation, operating mainly in Matebeleland, in the north-western part of the country. The apartheid security forces were already actively, if somewhat covertly, assisting the Rhodesian forces in order to stop the liberation war coming to its doorstep.

Also in existence at the time was a phalanx of hostile states that formed a barrier against the liberators. Angola in the west and Mozambique in the east were under Portuguese colonial rule. Namibia, until then administered under a United Nations mandate, had been annexed by the apartheid regime, which made it its fifth province, called South West Africa. Botswana, never hostile to the South African liberation struggle as such, was nevertheless too economically dependent on the apartheid regime and constrained by its threat of military reprisals should the country be seen to be supporting the ANC.

Ranged against those odds, it made sense that the ANC and Zapu should make common cause and fight together.

There could have been no mistaking the determination and high level of morale among the well-trained MK and Zipra guerrillas – Chris Hani, Andries Motsepe, Ntsimbikayigobi from Delmas, etc. among them – who had been selected for what later came to be known as the Wankie Operation. They couldn't wait to cross the Zambezi River and show their mettle in the war theatre. Given assurance of the adequacy of the preparations, Comrade O. R. gave the mission the green light.

And how magnificently the combined force acquitted itself! Their fierce battle execution was acknowledged by the enemy, which, in its dispatches from the frontline, reported that a 'new kind of "terrorist" who doesn't shoot and run away had entered the country'. Outstanding courage was displayed and some battles won, but the campaign eventually fizzled out – inevitably, given the strategy adopted.

Following the 1969 Morogoro Conference, I had the privilege of being appointed as Comrade O. R.'s secretary. There, I was in the shadow of a man who spent his waking hours thinking, writing about and executing the struggle for liberation in so many ways. Not only did he mobilise support for MK by securing training facilities, equipment, funds and complex logistical backing, he also rallied support from ordinary people in nearly all of the countries of the world for the diplomatic, economic, cultural and sports isolation of the abhorrent apartheid regime. Anti-apartheid movements mushroomed and sprouted up across the world. O. R. formed a close friendship with Olof Palme, the long-serving Swedish prime minister and won significant support from the people of Sweden and other Scandinavian countries who became the biggest financial/material/technical contributors to the struggle for our liberation.

President O. R. Tambo's humanity and total commitment to the liberation of the people of South Africa knew no limits. In closing the ANC Consultative Conference in Kabwe, Zambia in 1985, he said:

> *Comrades, my health has not been of the best lately. But what's left of it will be consumed in struggle.*

In fact, he gave his all for the liberation of our country and the democracy so many now take for granted.

He was inimitable.

Mavuso Msimang

PREFACE
He became the magnet that held the movement together

The Department of Arts and Culture (DAC) is truly proud to assist in publishing this collection of letters written by children of the struggle in exile to the longest-serving President of the African National Congress (ANC), Oliver Reginald Tambo. O. R., as he was affectionately known, was a selfless giant, a man of integrity, deeply religious, a seasoned intellectual, a science scholar, a teacher, a lawyer, and the embodiment of the National Democratic Revolution. The DAC therefore supports this endeavour to publish those letters so that generations to come may understand what he stood for, the pivotal role he played in the struggle for national liberation, and how he contributed to shaping the history of South Africa.

Reading these letters will help to increase the understanding of, and appreciation for, O. R.'s leadership in the process of liberating the country and its people, his passion for people and belief in putting their needs first, his capacity to understand and diffuse difficult situations and nurture harmony, and his ability to communicate persuasively and unpack complex messages for the global community.

He valued unity, collective leadership, humility, honesty, discipline, hard work, internal debates, constructive criticism and self-criticism, and mutual respect. His simplicity, his nurturing style, his genuine respect for others, and his willingness to listen to all people brought out the best in them. Like a good father, he valued education and raised funds to provide schooling and shelter for young exiles to ensure that they completed their education before joining the military struggle. For serious and deserving scholars, he not only provided bursaries, he placed them in friendly countries around the world to further their studies.

He led the ANC during the difficult years, which meant coping with the prevailing uncertainty, loneliness and homesickness. He became the magnet that held the movement together during the most turbulent times and frustrating years in exile. His genuine commitment, insight, understanding and ability to articulate the ANC's vision and mission enhanced our course in the eyes of the international community.

O. R.'s early, humble life and his traditional rural roots moulded his style in politics and leadership, and while the expertise he acquired through education and experience was very different, he combined them creatively to develop an approach that reached and empowered a broad range of people, both nationally and internationally. The values and life skills he inculcated enabled him to make an enormous contribution to, and to have an enduring impact on, the history of the ANC and the new democratic South Africa.

Mr Nathi Mthethwa
Minister of Arts and Culture

ENDORSEMENT
Seen through the eyes of the hopeful and trusting children

This book comes at a time when South Africa most needs to hear the voices of those who grew up with, lived with and learnt from Oliver Tambo.

Conversations with Uncle O. R. Tambo presents a unique opportunity for the reader to get a glimpse of the thoughts, aspirations, trepidations and regrets held by those who experienced and grew up under O. R. as children in exile. Their stories bring to life the reality of exile as seen through the eyes of the hopeful and trusting children who, as adults, 30 years on, take a moment to reflect on their relationship with uncle O. R.

Those are South Africans who, as children, started schooling in exile under the leadership, support and influence of O. R. Most got to know of him through their parents, while others got a chance to talk, touch and play with him. What is common among them all is the respect and love they had for him. They believed in and trusted his vision, such that most shaped their lives to contribute to his dream, and some chose careers they never thought they would achieve persuaded by his passion for education and a skilled cohort of leaders ready to take South Africa to the next level: post-apartheid. There is a famous line that O. R. often used that said: when liberation comes, South Africa will require educated, skilled people to lead various sectors of state and society. Education was central in all of O. R.'s engagement with children in exile.

Although some didn't wanted to study but instead wanted to train as soldiers to fight the apartheid regime, O. R. insisted on their education, hinting at what type of leaders would they be if they did not study! So that became the central focus of most children's lives as they endured the suffering of exile and isolation from loved ones back home. They attended school, went on to study at universities across the world, lost parents, friends and uncles, but never lost hope for a free and democratic South Africa.

The Foundation is pleased to be part of the *Conversations with Uncle O. R. Tambo* initiative contributing to the O. R. legacy stories we collect and record. Contributions from this book will be used to support and sustain the Foundation's work in education as well as work with youth in communities. The programme aims to, among others, instill a value-based lifestyle for young people in and out of school. These letters will, among other things, be used to inform and motivate young people to trust in their inner self and their ability to aspire to a future in which they are the architectures of their destiny.

The Foundation is indebted to Ambassador Lindiwe Mabuza for initiating this project and dedicating the proceeds to the Foundation.

Linda Vilakazi
CEO of the Oliver and Adelaide Tambo Foundation

O. R.'s LEGACY
A duty to fight for the legacy

This significant contribution to the South African political history, through letters and photographs, is the realisation of the passion and commitment of Ambassador Lindiwe Mabuza.

In giving fresh insight through the writings of his political children into the life of President of the African National Congress, Dr Reginald Tambo, this book reminds us all of his sacrifices, joyful moments and his values.

It is my pleasure to have been asked to comment briefly on this important initiative. My hope is that at this crucial moment in the history of South Africa, this collection will remind us and the international community of the achievements that have been made. It is a reminder that the fight for the liberation of our country, as my mother Dr Adelaide Tambo once said, is not quite done. It is a reminder that all South Africans have a duty to fight for the legacy left to us by our many fallen heroes.

Finally it is a reminder that we must forge ahead together to ensure that future generations continue to enjoy the country that belongs to them.

Nomathemba Tambo
South African Ambassador – Italy

MEMORY IS *our* heritage™

Power tends to corrupt, and absolute power corrupts absolutely. Great men are almost always bad men – even when they exercise influence and not authority – still more when you superadd the tendency or certainty of corruption by authority.

Lord Acton, 8th Baronet, John Emerich Edward Dalberg-Acton, April 1887, in a letter to Mandell Creighton, an Anglican Church scholar.

Back in 2000 while conducting research into the enigma that was the leader, in Oliver Reginald Tambo, having interviewed his contemporaries, such as the late fellow mathematician Dr K. W. Kambule, Fort Harian and partner in the law firm Mandela-Tambo, their colleagues and ex-lecturer at the University of Fort Hare and his Baa Baa Sheep protege and later High Court jurist, Judge Fikile Bam, I sought guidance from my literary and spiritual inspiration and Baba – apart from Ntate Prof Es'kia Mphahlele – the lively and animated Professor Baba Raymond Mazisi Kunene, democratic SA's first National Poet Laureate. A! Baba! Ancient Hero of the Ages.

I had gathered enough pluck to ask him, as National Imbongi, to put pen to paper to unpack who O. R. really was. Telephonically, he told me this and that, and yet some more. And I replied,

'Kindly put it down in writing, Baba. I hear you, but still I do not comprehend the meaning. I do not wish to misquote you, Ntate Kunene.'

'Ahh, *uyahlupha*, Mothobi, he argued. When would you want it? Tonight', I replied naughtily but added the rider: 'tomorrow would not be too late, either.'

True to his word, Professor Kunene delivered on his promise, unlike most politicians worldwide who promise you the world when they cannot even deliver a comprehensible speech.

I digress.

Early before the first cock crowed, I heard the fax copier announcing proudly, t-t-TtTT – hear me, hear me, here I come, *mfowethu*: typed by Bab Kunene himself. I knew I had been blessed and I cried in joy and humility inside and called our national poet, '*Ngiyabonga*, Baba.'

'Are you happy?' he asked. Tongue-tied, I muffled, 'Yes,' and a louder 'YESS!' 'Well, I have never shared this intimate portrait of

A TRIBUTE

Prof Mazisi Kunene

The Story That Had to be Told

It is not easy to write and talk about someone like O.R. Tambo (as he reverentially addressed). Yet I know within myself that he would approve that this text about him I could or should write about him. I do so with confidence that his spirit would guide and instruct me where he would feel necessary. O.R. was older than me. This is a reference that will explain the level of understanding and comment about him as I knew and understood him. First and foremost I must state that I write about O.R. with a sense of reverence. This sense does not only refer to the period as redefined by memory and the many accolades that have followed his life's achievement but the period I interacted with him. The period describes the era of O.R. when he was not only my leader but my commander. In short, I respected and adhered to his command. As I explained in the eranse of my interrogation: "If Tambo had told me to jump from the top of a multiple story building, in the name of the ANC, I would have jumped. I would do so not out of blind obedience but because I would assume that he would have calculated that the act would save so many comrades". Yet to do so would be an extreme act of commitment to our cause, requiring such ultimate sacrifice for our liberation. In other words no action of Tambo would ever (or was ever) or would ever be committed out of sheer selfish motives to gain a score for his leadership. He was a person who would share equally the risks, the lifestyle, with all the comrades. He lived a simple personal life and slept in a simple rickety bed in the camps which I myself once shared with him. It is necessary to refer to these aspects because they tell us about the man as he truly was. Not as described by those who only partially understood his parental concerns. It is necessary to refer to these aspects from the earliest episodes of Tambo's life in exile so that we can better grasp the source of elements that made Tambo, Tambo. In other words we must understand Tambo not at the moment when his scope and leadership projects him as a mountain. For indeed, it is easy to praise and be overwhelmed by the size and scale of the mountain without understanding the rocks and pebbles that make up the mountain. Our desire is, will always be, to allow generations and generations to understand the quality that

1

O. R. with anyone else before,' he said. 'I also wish to thank you for having bothered me. Let me go back to sleep lest I disturb MaThabo.'

Later in the day, I further prodded Baba Kunene: what were some of the ingredients of O. R.'s leadership skills? Spirituality, integrity and the humility he learned from his mothers – his father's wife – which balanced him in all his dealings with people, giving the ability to listen and empathise and not parade his gender.

He placed his whole affection and ambition in those purer speculations where there can be no reference to the vulgar needs of life, according to Plutarch.

And his last words are reportedly:

I beg of you, do not disturb these circles.

When were these quotations first uttered? And who were they referring to? Definitely a mathematician.

But who?

Well, let us end the mystery.

They were first spoken - at least – more than a thousand years ago – before Christ.

The mathematician in question is echoed in the legacy of the humble icon we are honouring in this book, the universal village boy from Bizana, and Teacher's Teacher, and Madiba's eternal bosom buddy and partner in law and in action, Oliver Reginald Tambo.

He too – like the Greek mathematician and scientist, Archimedes – Uncle O. R., as the young contributors in *Conversations* refer to him with affection and honour – was a persistent if not consistent problem solver. That to every question there is an answer, however complex the challenge might be. And that it is our purpose in life to solve each and every problem life throws at us, even if it takes us a lifetime.

That is the sum total of the writings to be found in this superb historical childhood memoir edited by Ambassador Dr Lindiwe Mabuza, a first of its kind in the African publishing world, if not in the southern hemisphere. Salute, I say, salute Editor Mabuza and the Magnificent Masupatsela a Tata Walter Sisulu. Salute!

It is clear what Perennial Problem Solver Uncle O. R. was creating constitute the myth. For indeed, lives of our heroes and heroines are well laid and well constructed by episodes. It is then easy for the dream that generations and generations will share and from it learn to evolve their own dreams. For liberators operate on a dream that far transcends their times and circumstances.

Therefore, to be able to understand properly one must learn to dream, learn to share it with others the Big Dream. Indeed, no dream is or can be of cosmic scale unless it is shared with the rest of humanity. In fairness to generations that will follow we must tell the story as it evolved. We must elaborate on the actors and actresses who make such story great. We who know and we who are witnesses that the leader if he or she is truly great shall be an embodiment not only of the pains of the era but also the joys emanating from the life of others for which the great sacrifices were made; or with whom they were made. That way we know that the chosen individuals, the Moses, the Kwame Krumahs, the Canon Collins, the Martin Luther Kings, the Albert Luthulis, the Patrice Lumumbas, the Ben Barkas, the Gamal Abdalah Nassers, the Ben Bellas, the Dr Moumes, the Steve Bikos, the Ruth Firsts, the Rosyln Endsleighs, and all the known and unknown heroes of humankind. All of them cared and shared a great dream for all human kind. For us and all generations they constitute countless galaxies of our vast and clear eternal skies.

It is for that reason that the story must be told. The story is not of one individual but of an era in which we lived, laughed and wept. We now must tell the story of Tambo who was chosen to be an embodiment of our journey throughout the night till sunrise. Hopefully there are many such stories that will be told what we know is that : "We Were Not Alone". But the question is what makes a hero a hero or heroine a heroine ? We are specially lucky to have gone through or are still going through a period in which will have create the Story. Other eras pass too quickly, too fast as a result we have no records of them, only the idea that they came and passed. But not Ours!

2

– the Next Generation of Leadership in the Young Pioneers, well in advance, from the time they were born! He had this educational vision, clear and unambiguous, for as one of the contributors puts it in the book – you have to buy the book to understand this assertion – *Education, education, education. Let us develop a culture of curiosity and learning.'*

That is the collective message from these young contributors, in probably a groundbreaking publication that in my 35 years of publication we dare ignore at our peril, for through their words, can we hear The Teacher's Teacher Voice of Uncle O R speaking to us in the present, for the future, since the past can never be reinvented as we chart a new path for ourselves, our country, and everyone else who calls this continent home. If you doubt me, do not hesitate to challenge me – after buying this book *Kalimera* (or *Kalinichta*).

Mothobi Mutloatse
2 December 2017

did a good job of succession planning, as you
ured that you groomed leaders who you could hand
the baton to.

Then there was the issue of your simple lifestyle... as we perceived it. As
office was said to be fairly modest. I specifically recall how you marveled at
At some point you rode around in a simple white Peugeot and had
luxury vehicle (possibly a black stretch limo) that had been offered to you

and responsibilities

you had time for us

and reminding us of

ge as well as our of

Dear Uncle OR,

I am the first-born daughter of

live with that tension every day

when my mother

weird and cold

school, we moved

names like Nthabiseng

having thought of myself as

Dear O.R....

Letter to O. R.

If I could write to the late O. R. Tambo, I would maybe say to him, 'I'm sure you still remember me. I first met you late in 1976 when you visited us as a group of students in a safe house in the suburb of Kinondoni in Dar es Salaam that served as a transit camp for ANC students waiting for scholarships abroad. I can still feel the buzz and excitement around the residence as you took the time to interview us individually, enquiring about our wellbeing, state of mind, and what had motivated our decision to leave our homes and go into exile. We were hugely impressed by your generosity of heart as you painstakingly listened to each one of us giddily reflecting on our experiences during the lead-up to the 16 June student uprisings. I remember thinking then that you probably had millions of other, more pressing, matters to attend to as the leader of our movement, rather than suffering through our rather naïve opinions and exuberant ideas. We knew about your punishing schedule and your numerous international commitments mobilising support for our struggle. As we shook hands at that first encounter, I remember your warm smile as you joked about my haircut – I had a fairly big Afro then, which placed me squarely in the black consciousness camp – slyly proposing that we swap our hair.

I remember that O. R.'s occasional visits to Dar were big events for everybody. When he was in town, there would be a noticeable change within the ANC community there. Whenever word circulated that O. R. was around, a lot of the ANC cadres who had, for years, virtually disappeared into obscurity in Dar would, so to speak, 'come out of the woodwork' and make themselves visible around the ANC Dar office, positioning themselves to be noticed by O. R. Suddenly those members of the National Executive who had practically absconded their responsibilities would be miraculously back at their desks looking busy. Such was the quiet authority of O. R.

With the growing turmoil in Soweto and other parts of the country, hundreds of youths poured into refugee camps in Swaziland and Botswana, and many swelled the ranks of the ANC. When my scholarship came up for study in the Soviet Union in 1976, I was asked to postpone it for a year to assist those students. In 1977, when I thought I had more or less completed that task, I approached the then ANC Chief Representative in Dar and put in my request to go for military training in Angola. I could not see myself sitting in Dar and waiting a whole year for a scholarship. So I had collected my paltry belongings together and was ready to join the next batch going to Angola, when I was called in by O. R. who had just returned to Dar from a visit to Nigeria and other West African states with offers of more scholarships from those countries for South African students to complete their high school education. When he learned that I had worked on scholarships, he wanted me to urgently prepare candidates to take those offers. I found myself more and more absorbed in scholarship work, and the plan to join MK was shelved indefinitely. During that time, I was persuaded of the idea that our struggle was not limited to the armed overthrow of the regime but extended to the building of a new democratic order that would require academically and technically trained cadres.

In August 1977, I finally received another offer for a scholarship in Moscow. I studied at the now Plekhanov Russian Academy of Economics where I graduated in 1987 with a Ph.D. in Economics. Several times during that period, O. R. Tambo came on official visits to the Soviet Union. It was during one of his visits to Moscow in 1984 when he drew me aside and personally conveyed his and the ANC's apologies and condolences on the passing of my brother Ben who was killed on 20 May 1984 as a result of a diabolical plot by agents of the regime who had infiltrated the movement. A sombre O. R. said to me that I needed to understand that there are unfortunately still such problems in our organisation and that the leadership was seriously grappling with them. He was visibly perturbed and showed genuine compassion and concern. Coming from him, that, for me, was a major source of comfort during that very painful time for our family. Those who

have had the honour and fortune of meeting O. R. could not fail to appreciate the greatness of that colossal figure whom history so prematurely, so unfairly, robbed us of on the eve of our democracy.

Bheki W. J. Langa

Dear Uncle O. R.,

I write this letter to you in a year that is earmarked by the African National Congress as one in which we celebrate you and your life achievements, as you would have been 100 years old. Conversely, in this year, I turned 55, and our non-racial democratic country reached its 22nd anniversary. I often think of you as I reflect on my own life path and wonder what would have been different in my life, our country, and the world if you had lived for at least another 25 years.

I am aware that how we live our lives is a culmination of the many different decisions we make and of the people who have a direct or indirect impact on our lives. There are the lessons learnt through my upbringing under education-embracing, internationally exposed, strict, loving, activist parents (Makhosazana and Wintshi Njobe who have sadly now passed on). You also impacted on my life in ways that I may not yet fully appreciate, as I was a child in the period in which we lived in Lusaka and a young member of society when you visited Mazimbu. What I know for sure is that your leadership style harnessed a sense of community and encouraged an appreciation for education and the practice of self-reliance in Lusaka and Mazimbu – places I lived in during our years of exile. Because of that environment, I could pursue agricultural studies in Bulgaria where I attained my degree in agricultural engineering, which

has been the bedrock of my continued personal growth and passion. My life was also shaped by the experience of living in Zambia as part of the exiled ANC community and working on the ANC Mazimbu and Chongela farms. I recall how, as a firm disciplinarian, you conducted ANC political and social gatherings in Lusaka and, during the one visit you made to Mazimbu, your interest in the detail about our Mazimbu farm and horticultural garden inspired me.

Uncle O. R., I am confident that, if you had lived to see us comfortably through the political transition to a democratic society, you would have steered, from exile, the ANC's evolution from a liberation movement with a domestic and international presence to a strong political party with a clear inclusive socio-economic agenda for South Africa, reflective of the aspirations of the people. I am convinced that if you had been the nation's first Black president, our approach to reconciliation would have been more attuned to the class issue in conjunction with the race issue.

Having had the honour, in the new dispensation, as the first Black female non-Afrikaans-speaking person under the age of 40 to serve as Director General in the Mandela and Mbeki dispensations, I could drive agricultural development and contribute to the African and international reintegration of a democratic South Africa in the same area. I believe that if you had been leading the ANC, our economic transformation agenda, guided by the aspirations expressed in the Freedom Charter, would have focused on ensuring that the agrarian reform agenda would have been driven by the desire for the land to belong to those who work it – Black and white. I realise that we might have tackled the agrarian reform challenges with a more deliberate appreciation for productivity and economic activity in the new South Africa, contributing to agricultural development on the African continent.

Sadly, things have not gone as well. This year, globalisation repeatedly raises its ugly and fear-inducing face covertly reversing the gains of the period when you were an activist for global peace. Even though we have agreed on Global Sustainable Development Goals, it appears that international solidarity is threatened by the diminishing visibility of transformational leaders who could act to stem the widening gap between the rich and the poor, mitigate political instability, eradicate corruption and ideological wars, and reinforce the imperative to nurture our natural and human resources for the greater good of society.

I lament your absence in our lives; however, I thank you for having been there, and I assure you that I personally know that much of

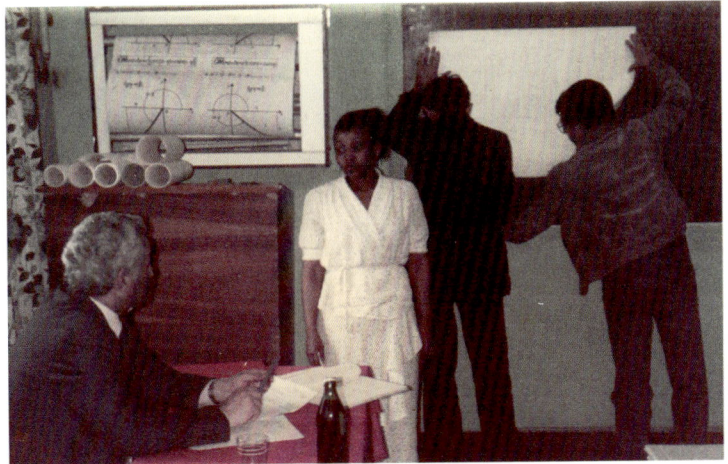

what I do is enriched by many aspects of which you were directly or indirectly involved. I continue to uphold the values and love for this beautiful country that I was raised in, and I seek ways in which I can contribute to its growth and development, consistent with the aspirations of the People's Charter of 1955.

Yours sincerely,

Bongiwe Njobe
(April 2017)

Dear Commander-in-Chief,

I am one of your many children who were in the bushes of Angola. I was very young and in my teens when I first heard about you. I was one born out of the 16 June uprising, but we started on the 21st, as I come from Kwa-Thema, the beautiful township near Springs. Yes sir, I know the townships are not places that we chose, but they are the ones that created many good and bad memories about who we are, where we come from, and where we wanted to go. That, to me, was the beautiful township because I knew every corner, and I have my lasting memories of my childhood there.

My parents named me Daisy Nompumelelo Tshiloane, and on my way to Angola, I had several names prior to my arrival in Luanda in July 1978, when Comrade Kitso gave me a name that formed who I became and is still a part of me: he called me Fortune Nala. Hmm, how I loved that name. In that name, I saw myself transform from a young girl to an artistic revolutionary.

The first time I heard about you was from my mother. I had already heard about Nelson Mandela and Walter Sisulu, and they were both in my photo album, but I had never heard anything about you. You see, I got myself involved in the student Black Consciousness Movement following the 16 June uprising. My mother heard about my activities in the township while she was working at the telephone-manufacturing factory. One of the teachers at a school that we visited – to mobilise the learners not to write while our student leaders were in prison – took a bus to where my mother was working and told her that her child was disrupting schools in the township. That was the only time I remember my mother coming home early from work. You see, I thought it would be treacherous to continue with examinations while our leaders were languishing in jail. When I ran home to do my chores before my parents got home – making the fire and cooking – I was startled by the door, which, surprisingly, was unlocked.

We normally left our key with Gogo next door, so I opened the door not knowing what to expect. Well, no one was in the kitchen, dining room or my bedroom, so I slowly opened my parents' bedroom, and there was Mum, in bed, obviously very unhappy. I was not used to having my mum home early from work, as that always made me feel I'd done something wrong if there were no pots on the stove. As I tried to close the door, she called me. I went in and realised that she was crying. I was touched. I had never seen my mother cry, unless she was praying. She asked me to sit down. I sat. She asked me about my having disturbed learners in schools. I wanted to lie but decided to go with the truth. I told her that some of our students had been arrested, including Fourie

Phakula who was our neighbour's son, and it could not be right that we continue as if nothing was wrong. When she asked me if I knew Nelson Mandela, I stood up to fetch my photo album and proudly showed her the picture of Mandela and Sisulu breaking stones. She asked me if I knew Oliver Tambo. I told her I had never heard of him. She then said that Mandela and Tambo were lawyers and said that Mandela was in prison and Tambo in exile.

I could not ask her where that exile was but thought that, if it wasn't guarded by police and soldiers, like a prison, I would go and see Oliver Tambo. She became emotional about my unwavering determination to continue. I did not say anything: she saw the defiance on my face, and she asked me what I had to challenge the boers with while big, strong, educated men languish in jail and others like them are in exile. I was never one to answer back to my parents, so I just kept quiet, but my heart was asking: how do we stop fighting when our leaders are in jail? Is that not part of selling them out? Will they not think that we have forgotten about them? I left the room with my mother nearly in tears again.

I asked some of my friends where that place called exile was, but none of them seemed to know. A few days after the talk with my mother, I got arrested. What was strange about that was the fact that Ntoanyane, a Special Branch boer who twitched every second

as he spoke, told me that I intended to go to exile with Tyson. I knew there was a Tyson who was one of the seniors, but I did not personally know him. I then thought someone was selling me out after my enquiries about exile, which I made because I wanted to meet with you, Sir; but who is Tyson, and how did he get involved in my going? I then resolved to find him so that he could take me along to exile.

The irony is that my mother ended up encouraging me to go to Swaziland. She knew that if I stayed, I would be tortured and maybe end up dead. I ended up meeting Tyson and other student leaders of the time who told Tiny Mthimunye and me to go for training so we could come back and fight with guns. The idea of going to learn how to use weapons excited me a great deal, and I swore that I would go and get trained to fight.

On our arrival in Angola, I was taken to Camp 13 for training: just imagine my excitement. I already knew a bit about you and had seen a picture or two of you in Mozambique and Swaziland.

I had gone through the transition of learning new words such as 'Comrade', which, in the beginning, I thought was someone's name because during my entire eight-month stay in Thokoza (Mbabane), I had never heard someone calling another, Comrade.

That is a story for when I meet you again. Let me go back to Quibaxe Camp 13.

I underwent my training, got 'cooked', got taught, and I became what I was proud of being (a trained MK guerrilla). Then came the graduation. Throughout the camp, there were preparations for the leadership who were coming, and in my heart, I hoped and wished, and was finally convinced that it was you who was coming for our graduation. I was part of the special platoon formed as flag bearers. Everyone wished to be part of that prestigious half guard. My sister Julinda and my mother Rachel were part of that platoon. We were four female comrades, including Mumsey Yedwa; the rest were male comrades and, all in all, we were about 18. We started making polish for our boots. You know, President, we were very resourceful those days for everything we needed but did not have: we improvised. I hope you won't be too disappointed to hear how dependent on others and the State we have become. I hope we get the chance to turn things around.

Now, back to Quibaxe. Comrade Phasha was busy training us as flag bearers to be on point and without fault. Then came the afternoon of 6 January 1979 when a convoy came through the main gates, the command to stand at attention was given, everyone stood at attention, and there you came – with other leaders, of course, but I wanted to see you. The command 'At ease!' was called as I looked at you and wondered how my mother came to know about you. I wished I could have shaken your hand. I had sung so many songs about you, and I had seen you, so my next wish was to shake your hand. That evening you stood in the queue for supper with us, but you were still so far away. Everyone wanted to talk to you. The day to follow was a Sunday: the day of our graduation.

In the culture of our camp, every month, individuals were recognised for discipline and acts of goodwill in the camp. They were called the 'vanguards of the month'. On the day of our graduation, guess who was the female vanguard of the month? If you can remember that day, it was a short, bony girl who was yours truly. That was after we had taken the oath, graduated, and been named the Isandlwana Detachment because you had named the year 1979 the year of Isandlwana because it was the centenary of the heroic and victorious war at Isandlwana.

Guess what? After holding the spear, I had to shake your hand as a vanguard. It felt like the whole day was only meant for me. I was a flag bearer; I took an oath; I graduated; I was named a vanguard, and I shook your hand. I wanted to go and sleep so that my tiny body could absorb all of that without me losing my mind. But my body was not ready for that: it was too excited to be put off to sleep. Fortunately, we had activities for the day, and the next morning, we got into the truck to accompany you to Fazenda Camp, where you went to talk to your soldiers. The same flagbearing process took place, as well as the taking of the oath by the soldiers. We drove back to Quibaxe, and the following day, we all stood at attention as you left. Some of our hearts sank, as we knew that when the leadership were around, there was good food, but when they left, we reverted to rice and *skop* or rice and *slava*.

The next time I met you, I was in the Amandla Cultural Ensemble, a group that was your brainchild. We had our rehearsal at Res One in Luanda. On that particular day, we were rehearsing a choral song, '*uMkhonto*'. Gracious me, I had no clue where you came from when you took over from Ndonda and conducted us. Everything we were previously taught took over without us even trying, and we smiled and observed crescendos as we pp'd and ff'd where the song prescribed. After uMkhonto, we went to Solomon Mahlangu, and that was the day I realised the beauty of that song. We sang like we were a concertina that opened and closed. After that, you greeted us and spoke to us about our importance in the struggle. You made us feel so special and chosen. Yes, we

always reminded ourselves that we were your special children and, believe you me, that is exactly how we felt.

On our first tour of the Scandinavian countries and West Germany, you kept appearing and disappearing. Oh, how that was a recharge to our souls. I remember when we first saw you in Holland, none of us knew that you were around, and as we were performing we saw you sitting in the front row. Off the stage, we asked each other if that was you and members of the rhythm section, who are always on stage, confirmed that it was you. The second part of the show was fire: the morale was just out of the place and that show was one of the very best I have ever experienced and performed in.

Then we went to Sweden. Was that part of the same tour or was it a later tour? I don't quite remember, but we were backstage ready to start the show while my mum, Lindiwe Mabuza, was on stage introducing the group. In her introduction, she acknowledged your presence in the audience. We became nervous and excited and the morale gauge soared from 60–110%. That was the effect of having our father at our show. Men and women alike were excited like little babies about to get a lollipop. Our singing, dancing, smiles, tears, poetry and everything that happened on that stage was priceless: we were just floating. At the end of the show, you always made a point of meeting us and telling us how great we were. We knew we were doing a good job, but to hear you say we were great gave us a power boost.

You kept telling us how special we were for the support we brought to our comrades on the frontlines and in the camps. You told us that what our Amandla group did in two hours took the ANC 20 years to accomplish. You do not know how we used that line in interviews. We quoted you every time there was a microphone in our face. We blew our own horn, and it felt good to quote you.

We saw it. We saw it in the Scandinavian countries where we collected clothing for our comrades in the camps with the NGO called Bread and Fishes. We saw it when we went back to Angola and were informed that Finland had sent buses to Mazimbu, Tanzania because we said we were students from the Solomon Mahlangu Freedom College. We got better food, we got more clothes, and we were told that we raised millions of dollars for our movement.

The next time we met with you was in the United Kingdom: the head of the serpent, as J. G. (Jonas Gwangwa) called it. We were hoping that one of our performances would be graced by your presence. We had already met members of your immediate family, which was strange, by the way, because you always belonged to us and we knew you as our father. So we wished that you would make one of those appearing and disappearing acts that we were so used to by now. You did not disappoint, and, as usual,

you spoke to us after the show to tell us how wonderful we were. With all the desertions that took place when people went abroad, we were expected to desert in numbers: in some of the countries we toured, we were put under immense pressure to leave the ANC and were offered beautifully furnished flats or condos, as they were called. We were told that we could stay in a bulletproof house with our family, and our children could go to expensive schools. We replied by saying that their children were not our leaders and were not forced to join the struggle because they were Tambo's, rather that joining the struggle was a personal choice, and no one was coerced. You kept us together. You made us look forward to another encounter with you. I was reminded that I had shared a stage with you in Scotland where I was invited to talk about South African women, as it was August, the month of South African women heroism. I was happy that I did not know you were there, as my excitement was going to get the best of me. Imagine how I felt when you were called to come and talk. I was in my early 20's and easily excited. You called me, shook my hand, and told me how proud you were of me. I swear I had a headache, or maybe shortness of breath, or maybe I had a malaria attack because I was sweating, and my hands were damp. I felt as if I were having an out of body experience. Then, we met with you again, on 2 November of that same year, in London, at the biggest march we have ever experienced. I don't know where the march started, but I remember we were singing all the way to Trafalgar Square passing 10 Downing Street. I was marching between Jesse Jackson and his wife and teaching them '90 Degrees Dolo Phezulu'.

On our arrival at the square, you came from nowhere and immediately all of us members of Amandla claimed you and wanted to protect you from the crowd by holding hands together and making a chain around you. We made sure that no one came too close. No one told us to do that, it just automatically happened when crowds saw you and went berserk: we just jumped in to make sure that you were safe. Oh, that was gratifying, and that was the last time we saw you in the UK. You saw us, and we were singing, and you gave us a knowing smile that said 'I see you'.

The next time we saw you, we were back in Angola, our home base, and you came to address us about the Nkomati Accord. We were happy to see you, as always, but as MK soldiers, the news of that accord was hard to accept, as we thought that the closing of that front was going to set us back years. You said that Samora Machel had signed his death warrant, and we would not be part of that funeral. You spoke about the apartheid regime wanting to share power and you said that power is not a bag of oranges to be shared out: one for me, one for you. We knew that withdrawing our forces from Mozambique was going to close one of our important fronts. That dealt our morale a blow, but you made us feel like there was a way around Nkomati and that we were going to intensify our struggle.

I know there are other encounters I had with you as an MK soldier and member of the Amandla Cultural Ensemble. Your name came to me through my mother's lips, and I feel so blessed to have had so many encounters with you, considering the large number of people who came to and then left Angola and other places without having met you. But I have met you and shaken your hand several times. In some instances, you hugged us. Those are memories that can never be taken away from me: they moulded the Fortune Nala who, in turn, passed it over to Daisy Nompumelelo Tshiloane. Meeting you and hearing you speak was like a religious experience that changes and forms perspectives. *Kennete haona yatshwanang lewena.*

'Til we meet again,
Tambo elihlab'elimzondayo

Daisy Nompumelelo Tshiloane

Dear Comrade Lindiwe,

I must say that I was surprised to get a message asking about my memories of O. R. Tambo. Why me? I thought; but all the same, I am pleased and indeed honoured to offer this.

My parents, Mannie and Babette Brown, met in Yeoville, Johannesburg in the early 1950s at a meeting of the Congress of Democrats, which was later integrated into the African National Congress. They fell in love, soon got married and, by 1959, had four children in tow.

Mannie was working in the underground structures of the South African Communist Party under the command of his lifelong friend, Joe Slovo, and Bram Fischer. He was instrumental in the escape from South Africa of several prominent ANC comrades, but it was his involvement in the escape of Rivonia trialists Abdulhay Jassat, Mosie Moolla, Arthur Goldreich, and Harold Wolpe that led to his imminent arrest and decision to leave South Africa and seek refuge in England. I often imagine now how exiles like my father coped with the news of the incarceration of the political activists they left behind, especially those they knew so well such as Bram Fischer, who eventually died in jail.

We grew up in a political family: one foot in the UK and the other at 'home' in South Africa. We marched against apartheid, held fundraisers, and handed out leaflets while our parents seemed to be less and less involved and more and more busy with the rigour of making a living and looking after us.

In 1982, in my mid-20s, I joined the ANC in my own right and found myself on a plane to Tanzania with an ANC delegation headed up by none other than Harold Wolpe. My job would be to take photographs of the movement's annual educational conference and to stay on at the ANC's school in Tanzania where I would work for several years as a photographer documenting the events in the region, building an archive and teaching others to photograph and print.

I imagined myself as the new revolutionary in the family, taking up the mantle where my parents had seemingly left off.

I remember vividly that one of the most momentous occasions in my time there at the Solomon Mahlangu Freedom College was the visit of the ANC President, Comrade Oliver Reginald Tambo.

I had seen him at rallies in London but always from afar. Here, at the school, his photograph was displayed everywhere, and even the little children knew his name and sang songs in his honour, and so his larger-than-life presence one day threw the young

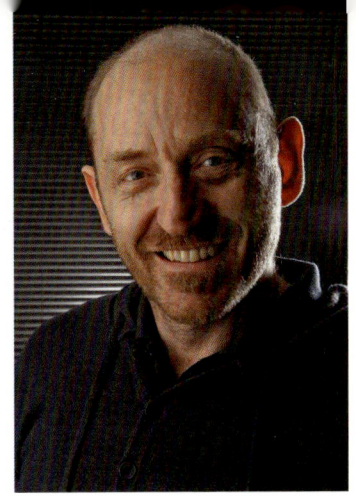

children into a frenzy of admiration. O. R. took a pen out of his pocket, held it high, and asked them if they could hear it drop. There was an immediate silence; the pen dropped; we all heard it; I let go of my breath; we all clapped, and I realised I had been so entranced that I hadn't taken a single photograph. O. R. then went on to open the new hospital, visit the farm, and tour the rest of the school, and I documented that, enthralled all the while by that wonderful man, his poise, and his respect for everyone he came across.

By mid-1990, most of the students in Tanzania were back home in a free South Africa and the ANC's school was handed over to the Tanzanian government. By that time, I was living in Swaziland with my then wife, Thandanani Dlamini, who had been an active member of MK, and our young son, Philani.

On a visit to London in 1995, my father told me how he had been running weapons into South Africa and had successfully supplied over 40 tons of arms to the ANC military wing, *uMkhonto we Sizwe*, in an operation called 'Africa Hinterland', which he had been spearheading from his flat in London under the command of well-known ANC leaders such as Aziz Pahad, Joe Slovo, Chris Hani and Cassius Maake. The operation was kept secret and no one was ever caught. I would eventually learn that the man at the centre of that intrigue was O. R. Tambo himself, the astute strategist with a finger on the pulse of the entire movement inside and outside of the country.

In 2000, I made a film about how those weapons were smuggled into South Africa under the seats of unsuspecting tourists in overland safari trucks. The film, dedicated to O. R. Tambo, is called the *Secret Safari* and is freely available for streaming or downloading on Vimeo at https://vimeo.com/193490599.

Attached are some of the photographs I took in Tanzania at the Solomon Mahlangu Freedom College, including some of O. R. Tambo's visit in mid-1984.

Long live the fighting spirit and wisdom of O. R. Tambo's African National Congress. Long Live!

David Brown

Dear Uncle O. R.,

My name is Jackie Motsepe. I was born in Lady Selborne. When I was four years old, our family went into exile, living in Zambia, Norway, the UK, Brussels, and Algeria. In December 1994, back in South Africa, my mother became ill and we came back to visit her. She subsequently passed away in January 1995. Then, after a short spell as South Africa's first ambassador to Ghana, my father passed away in 1998.

Growing up in exile, we learnt from an early age to develop an instinct for survival. Danger seemed a moment away. We knew our telephone conversations were being listened to. We could hear the crackling and distortions on the line and deduced that, 'They are taping us,' or 'They are listening.' 'We KNOW you are listening,' we would taunt. Somehow, we knew never to take the same route home. When our Father had to go away, I was always entrusted with the information of where he would be going, always for some work for the struggle: 'But you must never say where he is!' I somehow knew that it was imperative that I kept that information to myself. Yes, that was in the UK. Yes, that was in Brussels. Yes, that was in exile. Yes, that was during apartheid.

The struggle consumed our lives. We would always hear stories of how things were 'at home'. We could only imagine home, as we never knew it. Yet, from far away, we felt as though we belonged

there. There were meetings and marches and more meetings, where freedom songs were sung. One day we would go home, although there were times when that seemed impossible. The older I became and the more I understood, the more it seemed that the apartheid system would never fall. And yet, one day we would go home. We remembered South Africa at big events where profound political speeches were delivered: 8 January, 16 June, and Diwali on 16 December. Those days were etched into our existence. *Amandla and Mayibuye iAfrika.*

Uncle O. R., we miss you. It seems you were always there. My parents loved and believed in the ANC and everything that it stood for. They admired you as a leader. I learnt about South Africa and the struggle from them. I always heard them referring to you in their conversations – to what you said and did. It always felt and sounded right. When you passed away, it felt like we had lost our North Star.

You moulded my thinking to the extent that I believed in the Freedom Charter that hung on the walls of all our homes – and do so, even today. I read what you wrote in *Sechaba*, listened to you on Radio Freedom, and participated in many demonstrations against apartheid. I believe in non-racism, which we lived as an exile community in the UK. I may be naïve, but I grew up with family from across the racial spectrum: from Uncle Abdul (Bam) and Uncle Albie (Sachs) to Aunt Maud (Phillips), Aunt Stephanie (Kemp), and Aunt Yoliswa (Modise). I felt loved, and I respected them as elders. When we went to your home in London, the bus driver knew exactly where we were going and who lived there: a kindly smile and reminder when we reached the stop. So many ordinary people in the UK supported the struggle for liberation that you led. When we commemorated 16 June and 8 January, the people in the UK commemorated with us, in solidarity. When we marched, we filled the streets of London, and our marches would be seen on the news; our leaders would tell the story of apartheid; the leaders of the Anti-apartheid Movement would explain why apartheid was a 'crime against humanity'. The documentaries on the BBC and ITV would reveal the horrors of apartheid, and the people knew: they were not lied to, and they cried with us. You led an impressive campaign against apartheid and mobilised people all over the world.

I always remember you smiling, Uncle O. R., and making us as children feel welcome, involved and loved. One of the few times you were on television in the UK, my parents called us to come quickly and watch, so we ran to the television, and it was you; that was a magical moment. I then began to understand how important you were in the world.

You appointed my father as the ANC Chief Representative to the Benelux countries. We lived in Brussels. It's then that I began to see the respect that you wielded. My parents would take us children along to some important meetings in very grand buildings in Brussels. There would be groups of very important people gathered for the occasion, which was to listen to you. They listened, and you could hear a pin drop.

We had many visitors to our home in Brussels. I remember Uncle Wolfie (Kodesh) came. Aunt Dulcie (September) also came to spend a week with us in the summer. The political conversations would go on long into the night.

In Brussels, our survival instincts went into overdrive. You would pick up the phone to dial and think that someone was there. Then you would think: no, don't be silly. When you finished the phone call and waited before hanging up, you would hear a 'click', and then you would hang up. The silence on the line felt sinister, eerie. The lock on the ANC office door was broken often. When my father would go to unlock the door, it would swing open; papers were tampered with. That was reported to the police: 'Maybe the area is not safe,' they would say. So the office was moved to a 'safer' location. Letters were never opened without pressing them first to feel for foreign objects, as letter bombs were known weapons.

Once, when my father was on the tram, someone snatched his briefcase as the doors opened and then ran off. Often, we would be driving and our car would be followed: we would turn; they would turn; we would take down the licence number and report it to the police. The hand of fear had gripped our family. My father often looked perplexed, slamming down the phone defiantly and clicking his tongue. He would never say who had been on the phone. We never asked. Then, one day, early in the morning, a gym bag was left at the door of the ANC office. My father looked at the bag, was immediately suspicious, and called the police. The whole area was evacuated. They found a bomb in the bag and

safely detonated it. Had it exploded, it would have done massive damage to the office and the neighbourhood. My father was the target: he worked alone at the ANC office in Brussels.

A few days later, they shot and killed Aunt Dulcie September as she opened the office door of the ANC office in Paris: she had the mail in her hand. Aunt Dulcie ... Who? Why? When will they be arrested? Those questions have never been answered. Aunt Dulcie's murder has not been avenged.

'Forget about apartheid,' they say, 'no one is interested anymore.' How come? Tell us first who murdered Aunt Dulcie September. Shots rang out as the ANC office in Brussels was fired at. My father had gone to see who was at the door after he had answered the intercom, and the voice said that he was a journalist and had come to do an interview. Again, my father was suspicious: no journalist had made an appointment to see him. So he approached the door cautiously and locked eyes with 'the journalist' who immediately raised his gun and started shooting. My father never froze, as he had done military training. Instead, he zigzagged as the bullets rained down around him. The first one just missed his head, at which the gun had been aimed, and he had a graze on the side of his face, either from the bullet or shrapnel. We know all of this because the attempted assassination failed, my father survived, and he told the story to the Truth and Reconciliation Commission. He was able to positively identify the shooter who was an ostrich farmer by the name of Joseph Klue.

Could that be the same man who shot and killed Aunt Dulcie? Was that the same man who planted the bomb at the ANC office in Brussels? Who else had that man tried to kill? We don't know. *Amandla*, we have the power. *Mayibuye*, we are back home. The freedom songs seem to ring hollow because we do not have answers to those questions. My father went to his grave after trying to seek justice for the attempt on his life. The man he positively identified is still farming ostriches in the Western Cape: he has never come forward.

Oh. Oh yes. Forget about apartheid! No one cares! No one is interested in what happened then!

The problem is that those incidents shattered our existence. My father had to go into safe keeping and move away from Brussels to return later. We went back to the UK. My Uncle Oscar called from South Africa, as he had heard something in the news. I could hear his voice in the distance, and I could hear the tapes. I couldn't tell him anything: just that everything was fine.

It was a difficult journey for our family, and, in particular, for my parents, after that episode. The truth is that thousands of us are sitting and holding the pain in our hands and hearts. We don't know where to put it, Uncle O. R.

In Brussels, we have been in the presence of people like Beyers Naude, Michael Lapsley and Father Mkhatshwa who came to tell the world about the evils of apartheid. I learnt a lot from those experiences and felt privileged. There are many questions that do not have answers, but one day we will know. I'm glad I've had the opportunity to speak up – and how better than through a letter to you.

I grew up to embrace the struggle fully and contribute in my own way. I learnt from you that we would fight to liberate South Africa and would all go back one day to rebuild the country.

You were right.

Jackie Motsepe

Dear Comrade President,

I first met you when I had hardly completed a decade of life. I was in absolute awe when I met you, not because I knew of your deeds or because I understood the importance of the work that you did. I was in awe because of the respect and discipline shown by the Comrades at the Solomon Mahlangu Freedom College and elsewhere. There was so much reverence, and not long afterwards, I did gain a full appreciation of what our movement and sacrifice were about. Things have since changed.

Comrade President, when you passed on and left us, I felt tremendous fear, confusion and heartache. I grew up knowing you as a hero among other heroes and heroines of our movement. You led – with a serious passion and discipline – the collective that brought us safely and peacefully to a much better South Africa: a South Africa that fully embraced all of its citizens with a promise of reparative prospects for the African. I feared the worst. Although I had grown some since my first encounter with you, your passing was a harsh experience for me at 14 years of age.

Brief background

Comrade President, mine has been a life in the movement since birth. The histories that inform my heritage – of both strife and illuminating the excellence of the African – have remained a dialectic that inspires my efforts as an activist today. My history did not begin with my birth. It began with those who came long before my emergence. Although it runs much further back, I will describe it from the times during which I knew my grandfather, Mark Shope. His daughter and my mother, Ntombi Shope, took up activism just like he did. She went further to be a cadre of *uMkonto we Sizwe* (MK) and then Chairperson of the ANC in Mpumalanga after the unbanning in 1990. My history and love for my movement, my home, run deep.

Today's political life

I was the political advisor in the Speaker's office under Speaker Max Sisulu in the 5th Parliament. We left in 2014. I enrolled at the Wits School of Governance for a postgraduate diploma in management (Public Finance and Economics stream). Comrade Sisulu joined the Wits School of Governance as a Ph.D. student and research fellow where I became his research assistant. I am now a student at the University of Sussex where I am studying for a Master of Arts: Global Political Economy and am currently a visiting student on a research placement under Dr Siphamandla Zondi at the University of Pretoria.

You see, Comrade President, my life has been one of activism and political consciousness derived from a long while before me. I am a child of the movement, and I ask only for one very urgent thing:

that you engage all of my heroes – including my grandfather and mother – who have left us and ask them to intervene in the current challenges facing our movement.

Regards,

John Mikatekiso Nelson Kubayi

SOMAFCO AND O. R. TAMBO
Some reminiscences with John Pampallis

1. Why did you choose the place?

I left SA in 1976, partly because I wanted to study further and because I was becoming increasingly more political and disenchanted with life in an apartheid society. I went to live in Canada because my girlfriend, now my wife, was a Canadian. As soon as I settled in to Winnipeg, I joined the Anti-apartheid Movement. I also registered as a master's student in education (I had previously qualified as a teacher in Durban and taught for two years – one in Durban and one in Botswana). A year after I got there, an ANC unit was established in Winnipeg and I became a member. Two years later, word came through the ANC structures that it was establishing a school in Tanzania and needed teachers. I applied to teach there and, in April 1980, went to Mazimbu with my wife, Karin, who worked in the construction administration for most of her time in Mazimbu.

2. What did you do?

I was a teacher of history and English. In my final year (1988), I was also head of the social science department and, for a year or two, I was the Staff Commissar, a sort of combination of political education officer and social welfare officer. In my final year at the school, I was a vice principal of the secondary school of Somafco. I also took part in the political structures at Mazimbu and was Chairperson of the (Mazimbu) Zonal Political Committee in 1988.

For a 15-month period in 1985–86, I went to London to write a history textbook for the school. It was printed by the ANC for use at Somafco and was later published as *Foundations of the New South Africa*.

I eventually left Somafco in January 1989 to go to the UK, where I worked for two years with Harold Wolpe and others doing research on SA education and preparing policy for the post-apartheid period.

3. Challenges

- When I first arrived at Somafco, the academic life of the school was quite chaotic. Students attended classes and evening study periods as they liked, classes were seldom full, and there didn't seem to be much that the school administration could do about that. The situation changed sometime in 1981 when the Student Council, realising that the situation was not benefiting anyone, took things into their own hands and began cooperating with the school administration to instil discipline and ensure that the school ran properly. From then on, the educational programmes ran fairly smoothly.

- Some of the students were quite disturbed as a result of being displaced from their homes in SA and having to get used to a completely different environment. Some had been traumatised by torture in South African prisons where they had been incarcerated before leaving the country. Mazimbu did not have the skilled personnel they required to deal adequately with that problem.

- Classes were composed of students of widely differing ages. In the upper classes, for example, students ranged from 17–23 years of age. A few students, including in the lower forms, were even older.

- In the early years, the infrastructure was very poor. Residential accommodation was crowded and inadequate for teachers and, especially, students. Food was basic but there was always enough of it. From my second year in Somafco, new houses were completed for staff and new dormitories completed for students.

- During the first year or two, students arrived at the school throughout the year and were admitted. That disrupted the teaching as new students kept joining classes with no knowledge of what the others had studied so far. Later, that was later remedied by keeping new students at Dakawa (another piece of land provided by the Tanzanian government about 50 kilometres away where a vocational training centre was built. In Dakawa, students received preparatory lessons and political education until the new academic year when they entered Somafco.

- During the early years, there was a shortage of educational resources of all sorts – textbooks, stationery, audio-visual resources, etc. For me, personally, one of the biggest problems was that there were no suitable books for South African history. The textbooks produced in South Africa were clearly unacceptable at a school of the liberation movement. I had to write detailed notes for my students (I was the only history teacher in the senior forms), so I had to do research using whatever books had been sent to the school library by anti-apartheid groups in various countries. Those notes later became the basis for the book I wrote later (see above). I also had to create notes for world history as we did not have enough textbooks to give the students.

- There was a shortage of teachers, especially for science and mathematics. After about two or three years, anti-apartheid groups in the Netherlands and other West European countries and the government of the GDR provided us with teachers for those subjects.

- There was a rapid turnover of teachers during the entire life of Somafco. Most teachers came from South Africa and had not had opportunities to pursue their higher education beyond a teacher's diploma or, at best, a bachelors degree. So as soon as they got to Somafco, they began to look for opportunities to go abroad to study. The ANC found such opportunities for them, but the result was a constantly changing teaching force. The foreign teachers who came on two- or three-year contracts were sometimes the most stable of the staff. Only a few South African teachers spent more than three or four years at the school.

4. Rewards

- I was at Somafco for eight years and, despite the challenges, found it very rewarding. I felt that I could contribute to the education of children and young adults who had been victims of apartheid. The school prepared several hundred young people for university or college education in various countries and they were later able to contribute their knowledge to a free South Africa.

- I got to meet and work with people from all over SA and also from other parts of the world. Those included students and teachers and also workers and various types of professionals because Mazimbu was much more than just a school. For the entire period of its existence as an ANC project, it was a building site: it also had small industries such as a furniture and woodwork factory and a garment factory. There was also a farm that produced crops and livestock, and there were supporting activities such as a health clinic (later a hospital), food supply services, maintenance teams, etc.

- I made some very close friends at Somafco, some of whom I still see regularly.

- Most of my political education took place at Somafco and for that I am very grateful. It also gave me the opportunity to meet ANC leaders such as O. R. Tambo, Moses Mabhida, Chris Hani, Ruth Mompati, Gertrude Shope, Mark Shope, Jack and Ray Simons, Thomas Nkobi, Alfred Nzo, Joe Slovo, Ruth First and others who all visited Mazimbu one or more times.

5. O. R. and Somafco

- I believe that O. R. was instrumental in establishing Somafco – i.e. in making the decision to establish the school and getting the Tanzanian government to make the land available. (That is not first-hand information but is what I was told by others when I was at Somafco.)

- O. R. visited Mazimbu on a number of occasions. I don't remember exactly how many, but I would estimate that it was an average of once every 18 months. He would spend much of his time with the leadership of the schools and the complex as a whole and would always make time to see and talk to students, teachers and other Comrades.

I can mention two anecdotes:

a) In the early months of Somafco, we had a school assembly every morning at which we sang the national anthem. When O. R. visited the school, I remember that he was uncomfortable about that practice. He felt that singing the national anthem so frequently cheapened it. His counsel was that the anthem should only be sung once a week at school assemblies and on special occasions. The school followed his advice.

b) As is well known, O. R. was very interested in education and had been a teacher when he was younger. Once, in about 1982 or 1983, he attended one of my English lessons. Of course the students were very excited and I was rather nervous. He was brought in by the principal (I think it was Tim Maseko at the time), but he stayed on his own and sat quietly at the back of the class for the entire lesson; we were almost unaware of his presence. At the end of the lesson, he thanked me and the students for allowing him to be there. He then spoke to me individually, told me that he had enjoyed the class and gave me some advice on what he thought could have made the lesson better. I don't remember the actual advice, but I do remember being grateful and impressed that he had taken that interest in my class.

John Pampallis
November 2017

Dear O. R.,

In the early morning of 17 March 1983, I arrived at the gate of Somafco. The setting was spectacular: mountains in the background, African bush wherever the eye could see, trees and cows. I was met by Comrade Tim Maseko, the principal of the school that would be my home for the years to come. Little did I know how those few years would change my life. Yes, I had travelled Africa. I had seen the roads and the villages. I had met the people. I had worked on the prevention and eradication of malaria. I had picked up the political motivation to fight apartheid. I had developed my solidarity with the supressed. But I hadn't stayed in a home with those who were my comrades in the struggle.

From that day onwards, I shared a kitchen and a bathroom. I shared the emotions of loneliness. Far from home. Far from loved ones. Committed to a political struggle. Sure! But no one could tell you for how long. No horizon. Nothing but 'within our lifetime'. I hoped my lifetime was still long. But I sure as hell didn't want the road to freedom to be as long. I was impatient. I saw Comrades leave. No questions asked. Where to? Friends that I got close to would simply disappear with no indications of where or when we would meet again. Somafco was a place of learning. And learning we did. All of us. About the topics at school. About life. About

ourselves. Because it was also a place of profound insecurity. Who can you trust? What is the truth? Do others see me as trustworthy? Where do we go? We had to invent and reinvent ourselves. A struggle. In all respects.

I left Somafco almost three years later. My life took a new turn. Three months after I arrived in Cameroon, where I started working in public health care, a colleague asked me: 'How do you like Cameroon?' I responded with no hesitation that my dominant emotion was that I was no longer at Somafco. I missed the determination, the solid belief in a better future, the discussions, the debates, the clashes, the sense of togetherness, and the collective. My life has been a long and winding road. I went left and right. But in my life, there has always been the sense that I had a life before Somafco and a life after that. I grew up at Somafco. I learned that there is no easy answer to the complexities of life. I learned that living together is an art. That you can understand others through the confrontation of belief structures, and that that only happens if you are open to it. I learned that politics is personal. That integrity has no political party.

I drove a motorbike at Somafco. It is called a piki-piki in Tanzanian

KiSwahili. My preference for pink outfits gave me the nickname 'Pinky Peter with his piki-piki'. The day that O. R. Tambo came to visit Somafco and indicated that he wanted to sit in on my class for an hour or so to see my performance as a teacher, Tim Maseko came to me in the morning and said: 'Hi, Pinky Peter, stop flying on your piki-piki; Comrade President wants to see you.' I slowed down and asked him if he thought I was worthy of such an important, high-level visitor. I could tell from his face that he had his doubts. But Comrade President had decided, so there was no way Tim could question the request. I was the proudest person in the school when the president commented on my teaching skills. He thought it was all prearranged and that I was informed beforehand that he was coming. That certainly wasn't the case. The whole visit was a pleasant surprise to me. But what came out, I guess, and was visible to O. R., was the interaction between the students and me. Inspiring and empowering: we were learning for life.

Peter Knoope (Piki-Piki)

Peter Knoope is a biologist who worked as a World Health Organisation-affiliated malaria researcher in Senegal, as a teacher in the Netherlands and as an educational advisor at the University of Nijmegen in the Netherlands before he came to Somafco. He joined other volunteer-teachers at Somafco from Sweden, East Germany, Finland and the Netherlands. He had to raise funds through his former biology students in the Netherlands to get proper biology books for his classes at the school. He speaks with great fondness of his highly motivated former students with whom he meets regularly in South Africa since deciding, in 2014, to live there.

A PHOTOGRAPHIC ESSAY OF SOMAFCO AND MAZIMBU BY DAVID MAX BROWN

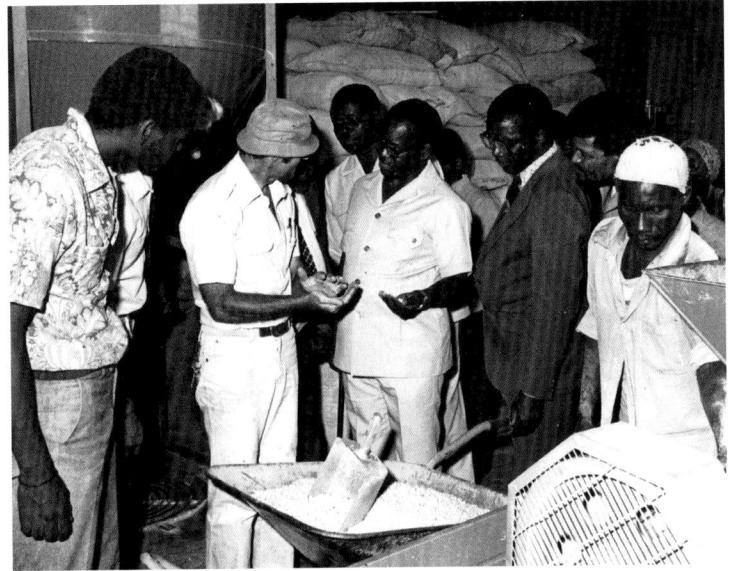

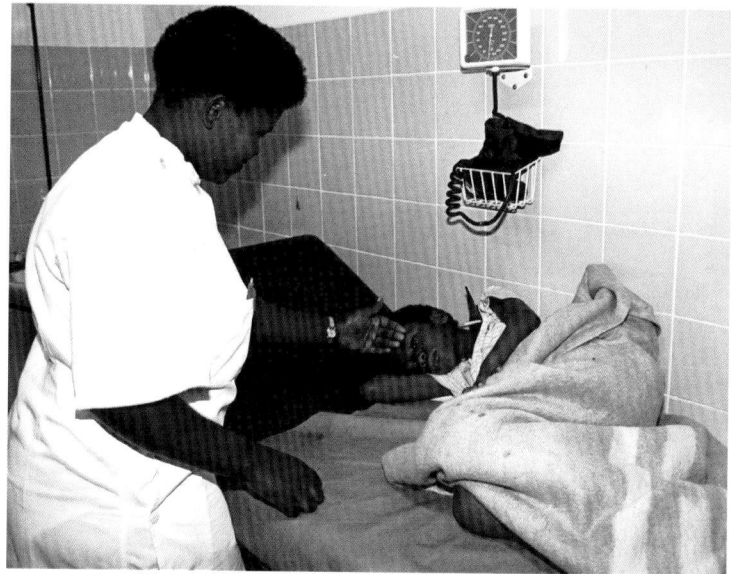

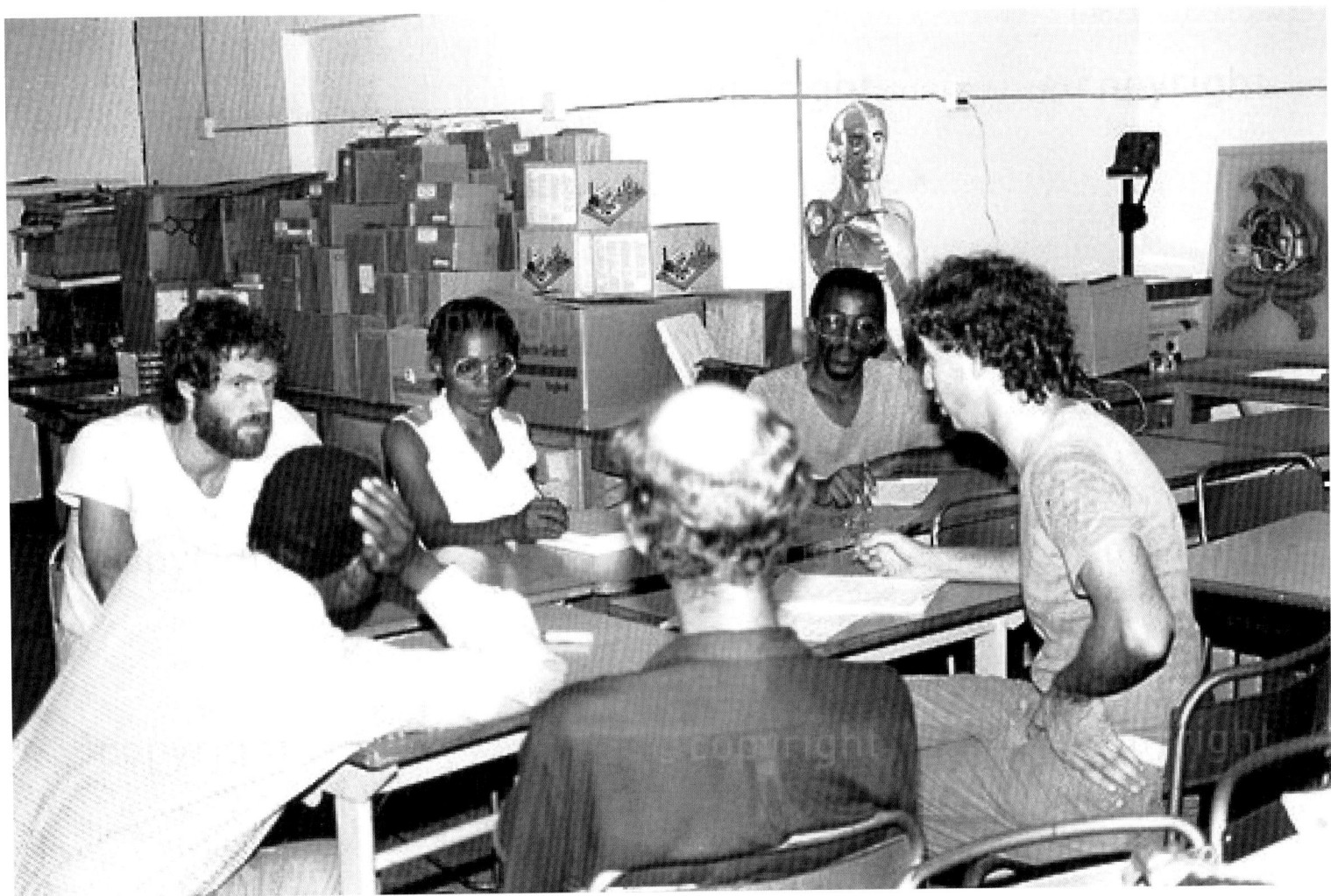

SOLOMON

The Solomon Mahlangu Freedom College is an educational institution established at Mazimbu, Tanzania by the African National Congress, the liberation movement of South Africa. The land at Mazimbu was granted to the ANC by the Tanzanian government. The school was designed to cater for the educational needs of the large number of students who left South Africa in the wake of the Soweto uprisings in 1976. Repression in South Africa continues to force our young people into exile.

Since the first foundations were laid in 1979 the ANC with the support and solidarity of the international community, has transformed SOMAFCO from an area of bush in a modern complex with a community of over 1200 people.

SOMAFCO is unique in that it caters for the complete spectrum of a community ranging from the care of young children to the education and technical training of an adult population.

Our lives at SOMAFCO and our educational policy are guided by our conception of the future South Africa that is envisaged in the ANC policy document, the Freedom Charter, especially its education clause 'The Doors of Learning and of Culture Shall be opened'.

THE DOORS OF LEARNING AND OF CULTURE SHALL BE OPENED!

The government shall discover, develop and encourage national talent for the enhancement of our cultural life;

All the cultural treasures of mankind shall be open to all, by free exchange of books, ideas and contact with other lands;

The aim of education shall be to teach the youth to love their people and their culture, to honour human brotherhood, liberty and peace;

Education shall be free, compulsory, universal and equal for all children;

Higher education and technical training shall be opened to all by means of state allowances and scholarships awarded on the basis of merit;

Adult illiteracy shall be ended by a mass state education plan;

Teachers shall have all the rights of other citizens;

The colour bar in cultural life, in sport and in education shall be abolished.

COSAS SUPPORT STUDENTS DEMANDS

SOLIDARITY

Progressive student organisations like COSAS, in South Africa continue to fight for the kind of education and student representation that is a reality for those in exile at SOMAFCO and which will one day soon become a reality for all in South Africa.

MAHLANGU

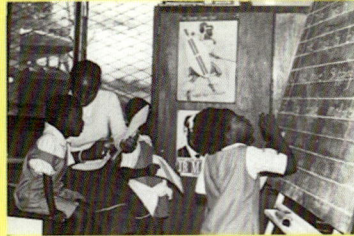

Education in South Africa is for subservience. At Mazimbu schooling is designed for liberation and to meet the needs of a future free South Africa. Contrary to Bantu education under apartheid, Somafco provides for all its students a full academic programme, which qualifies them for further training at universities or technical level in Africa or abroad. Emphasis is laid on teaching development of societies and the history of the struggle for freedom in Southern Africa. By integrating academic and vocational training, we aim to bridge the gap between mental and manual labour.

Initially conceived as a secondary school, Somafco now comprises five educational sectors: secondary, primary, nursery, adult education and a student orientation centre. In primary education much emphasis is laid on English, the language of instruction at the school, and on creating a consciousness of our cultural heritage and resistance to apartheid. Adult education concentrates on literacy classes, to enable unschooled members to play a more useful role in the community and to improve their skills. New arriving students are received and assessed for entry to Somafco in the student orientation centre, based at the new Dakawa, 50 km from Mazimbu. The students live in tents and classes are held in the open.

LONG LIVE CCM-ANC
FRIENDSHIP AND SOLIDARITY

___ is a school for young South Africans who have fled their country and faced many hardships. ___ is also an unusual community where all the students, parents, teachers, ancillary staff and workers live and work together on the same campus. This situation necessitates not only the continuous running of the school and all supporting structures, but also the organisation of all other aspects of daily life. The work in the agricultural and industrial sectors, the catering, sport and cultural activities, and the manifold political activities which play a crucial role in the community. All of us wish to go back to our homes in South Africa. Nonetheless ___ is a place which we are proud of as an embryo of the future South Africa.

___ is a monument to the SOLIDARITY that exists between the oppressed people of South Africa and the international community. As SOMAFCO flourishes and the ___ grows, financial support and material assistance from the international community and the peoples of Tanzania continue to form a crucial pillar in the struggle of the ___ for liberation, justice and peace in the South Africa of tomorrow.

COLLEGE

SOLOMON MAHLANGU FREEDOM COLLEGE

ANC

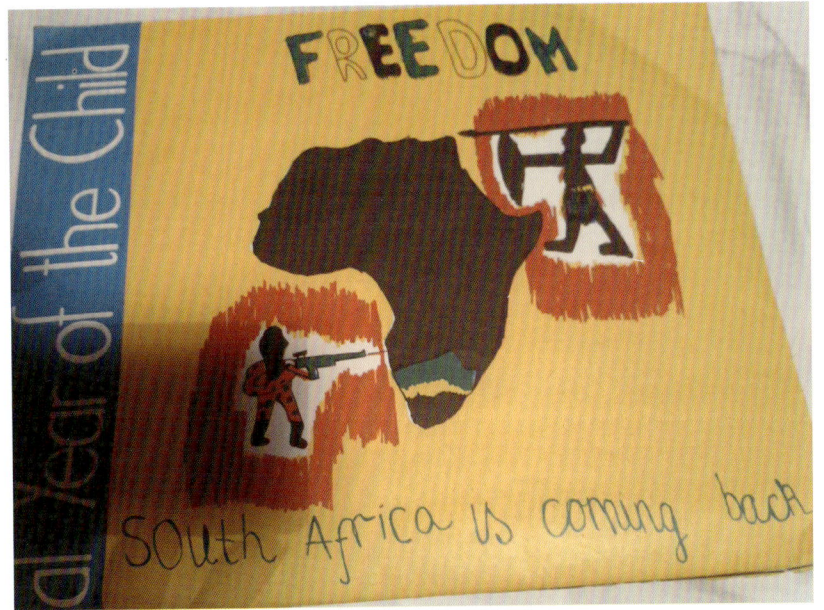

Dear Comrade President,

My mother tells me that you wanted to meet my sister and me following the 9 December 1982 Maseru, Lesotho cross-border raid by the South African Defence Force (SADF). As you know, that was the biggest raid of its kind, where 42 people were brutally murdered by the boers. Thirty of those people were MK cadres who had sought refuge in Lesotho where they were being trained as part of the armed struggle. I suspect the experience of having to clean their bodies was what made my mother an overnight vegetarian. I've never had the courage to ask her. I wonder if you ever discussed the physical brutality of it all with her and others. Twelve Basotho nationals were brutally killed on that night as well, including one of our neighbours who was shot for simply peering out of her bedroom window to see what the racket was about. She left behind a newborn baby.

I was badly injured, and I suspect that my life of activism and rebellion against an unjust society started on that morning at 1 a.m. when I was woken up by a noise I'd never heard, a smell of metal I had never smelt, and a fire I never thought I would ever witness, despite the fire drills at primary school. I was eight years old. My hero, my father, resembled Rambo that night with ammunition across his chest and an AK-47 in his hands. As far back as I can remember, he had prepared us for such a moment: we knew to stomach crawl, the way he had trained us, and to stay totally silent. What saved our lives was when he stopped shooting back and the boers took us for dead. We stayed in a burning house for what seemed like hours before my dad felt we were safe.

The saddest thing, for me, in the aftermath of that raid, was the whispers of comrades who said that the only reason we survived was that my father was a spy. I only heard of those whispers as an adult, and I struggle to have functional friendships with the offspring of those comrades who socialise in my circles today. Their cruel fathers are now dead. Those accusations and innuendos broke my dad and continue to have an effect on him today – although we don't talk about it. I have read in his 'When I Resign from the ANC' letter on the Internet, and been told by those who remain family friends and Comrades, that it was through your intervention that he was not killed by witch hunters whom I suspect were settling other scores through those accusations. Some among them are the biggest looters today, bringing our movement into disrepute and sadly proving that some among us are not fit to govern South Africa.

I recently wrote an open letter to our recently departed Seaparankwe Ahmed Kathrada, Uncle Kathy, days after we laid him to rest. It was my final letter to a Rivonia trialist following an exchange of a series of published letters to the surviving Rivonia

trialists in 2012. At the time, it was President Nelson Mandela, Seaparankwes Denis Goldberg, Andrew Mlangeni, and Uncle Kathy. Tata Mandela was way too ill to respond, but his foundation took note of the letter.

The initial letter I wrote was lamenting the state of the ANC at the time – and particularly the quality of leadership – as the movement prepared for its 53rd National Conference in Mangaung. At the 52nd conference in Polokwane, populists with varying interests had pushed for a rape-accused former deputy president of the country whose car washes were being paid for by someone he had a generally corrupt relationship with. I know you knew Uncle Judson Kuzwayo. His daughter, my former classmate, dear sister, and friend passed on eight months ago after 12 years of insisting that Jacob Zuma allegedly raped her*. His blind supporters made her life a living hell until she decided to silently give up on life in this world. I hope that, as an ancestor, like you – she has found peace.

Our government and movement have been captured by an immigrant peasant family from India: the Guptas. This year of 2017 was dubbed a year of unity in your name. I find it an insult to sully your name in such a manner after all of your efforts to try to keep the ANC united and functional during the decades in which

you were our president. President Zuma urinates on your legacy daily with his handlers.

Anyway. Let me conclude with this thought: Some time back, society rebelled on a Friday and took a day of action to protest state capture. I participated in an illegal but peaceful protest outside of the home of the Indian peasants who live in the plush suburb of Saxonwold. Everything about them, save for the suburb of their choice, proves that money doesn't buy class. The South African Police Service was on the scene like a mini army. At some point, they attacked us protestors – whose only crime was to hold protest signs – with stun grenades, tear gas and rubber bullets. I ran away with my fellow protestors, but something made me go back and refuse to move. That was the day that I knew that our struggle is far from over, and that if need be, I am willing to die for a free South Africa.

Kananelo Sexwale

*Ed. note: Jacob Zuma was acquitted of the charge of rape

Dear Comrade President,

I was born and grew up in Durban but left to go to the UK in 1975 at the age of 12. I was not an exile in the traditional sense, having had no overtly political reason for leaving South Africa. I was relatively politically unaware at that time, yet I knew innately that apartheid was fundamentally wrong. Segregated social and recreational facilities made no sense to a 12-year-old! The contrast with the move to an integrated society in an inner-London school with children of all races (despite its racial prejudices) could not be more stark.

But I was far from home, feeling distant and alienated from what was happening inside the country. I followed what was happening at home, maintaining regular contact with family and friends. I read as much as I could find, including copies of *Sechaba*, which opened my eyes to the African National Congress and you, Comrade O. R. Tambo. Its ideals resonated with me and I was drawn to its vision of a non-racial democratic South Africa.

In the 1980s, I found myself studying law at Southampton University, which was my initial contact with the ANC when a speaker from the London ANC office (George Johannes) came to address a meeting. That interaction led me to discover a new family of South Africans within the ANC who embraced me, taught me and nurtured me. My family and friends were extremely supportive of my desire to associate with an organisation that was executing the noble struggle against racism and apartheid. The ANC had won the respect of many people across the world, due, in no small part, to your exemplary leadership.

When I completed my studies, I gravitated closer to the ANC and was soon working at its London office. I was fortunate to be present at both of the Wembley Stadium concerts in honour of Madiba in 1988 and 1990. However, my fondest memory of that time was the day in April 1990 when the staff from the ANC London office accompanied you and Madiba to a private viewing of a statue of Madiba at Madame Tussaud's. I will never forget how the two of you laughed like naughty schoolboys when you saw the waxwork image, with Madiba asking of the statue, 'Why is that chap not smiling?'

With the African National Congress having declared 2017 as the Year of Oliver Reginald Tambo to commemorate the century of your birth, you have been in the minds of many, many of our people these past few months. As the challenges faced by the peoples' movement grow exponentially, the vision, wisdom, guidance and leadership that you and many of your generation of venerable leaders provided, is sorely missed. Your name and legacy is all too often invoked in vain, and, on many occasions, it is done in a manner that fundamentally contradicts the culture of engagement and contestation of ideas that you promoted. A municipality with atrocious records of governance, administration and service delivery carries your name.

It is hard to comprehend that, in a little over two decades since 1994, a period that almost matches your tenure as president of our movement, we have regressed so far, and that we now witness ugly public spats between erstwhile Comrades. People who shared the battle trenches against the vile apartheid regime now find themselves in opposing trenches. We are separated between, on the one hand, those who are willing to undermine the sacrifices of our movement in naked pursuit of personal enrichment, and on the other hand, those who remain firmly committed to the values of the liberation struggle. Those values of selflessness, equality, human dignity and freedom epitomised the ANC that I knew under your leadership. Those were the principles that sustained us during those dark days in exile.

The struggle for national liberation was premised on the notions of justice and equality: that a democratic society is sustained by the rule of law under which we are all equal. It represents a fundamental rejection of apartheid, which treated people

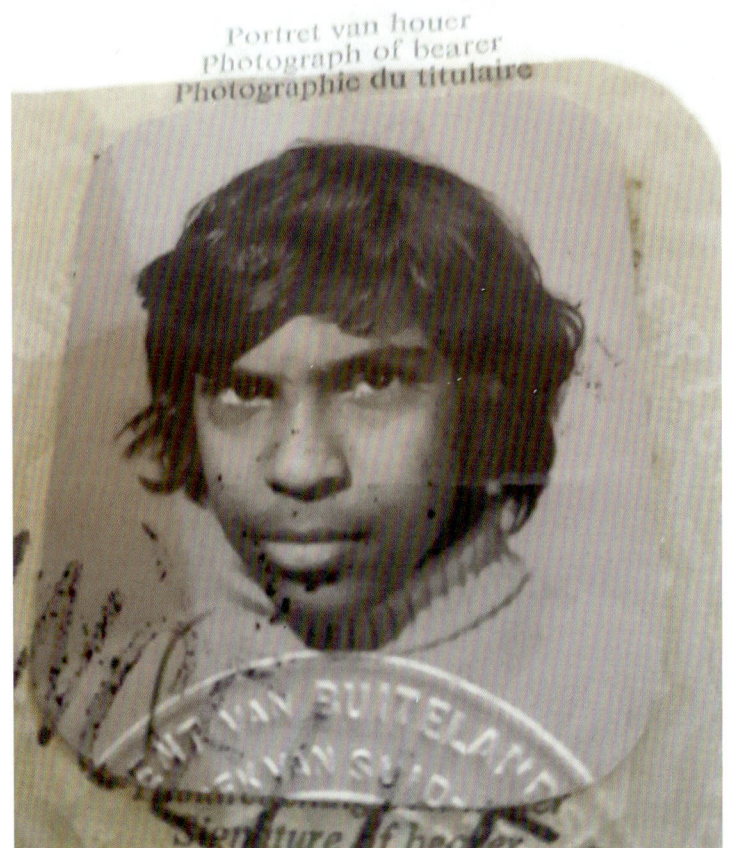

Portret van houer
Photograph of bearer
Photographie du titulaire

differently based on the colour of their skin. The rule of law itself is underpinned by an independent judiciary that is free of political manipulation. Yet, we now see brazen attacks against members of the judiciary when they make rulings against organs of state that have violated the constitution, the law, and the social compact, which comprise the foundation of our democracy. We now have a ruling elite abusing the banner of the African National Congress so as to usurp power from the people. That is the antithesis of what the ANC fought for.

ANC members are now commodities that are traded. Branches are now simply bought by people with money in order to exert improper influence over the government. I am reminded of the process under which I became a member of the African National Congress. I attended an interview on a cold Saturday morning in London with three veterans of the struggle. I was nervous, somewhat intimidated, but mostly daunted. I questioned whether I was worthy of belonging to an organisation that I held in such awe. Could I ever hope to live up to the example set by you and others of your ilk?

I was fortunate, Comrade President, to have been able to spend some time with you in the early 1990s when you were recuperating from your stroke in London. I visited you in Muswell Hill for lunch a few times with other Comrades. Discussions always focused on developments inside the country, the challenges being faced and how the mass democratic movement could overcome them. You were always more interested in listening to our thoughts on those major issues than giving us your views.

If only our leaders now would listen.

Comradely greetings to you and the ANC branch in Heaven,

Lawson Naidoo
Cape Town, 9 May 2017

O. R. Tambo,

It was an early morning weekday as I opened the gate and my father maneuvered the car along the narrow driveway out of the yard onto the main road, a semi-circle crescent that surrounded an open field as you exited. In the distance in front of us, 500 metres away and beyond the open space, was Garden Compound, a typical equivalent to a 'township', one of the sprawling and densely populated settlements in the city of Lusaka.

Something seemed different that morning as we prepared for the drive to school. On the horizon, clouds of dust billowed above the shack-like houses as some strange flying objects hung suspended over the settlement, like UFOs. They seemed to be dropping hundreds of tiny speck-sized objects, which slowly fluttered and fell to the ground. Then, like a swarm of hornets, those flying things seemed to come straight towards us, but wait! Those look like rotors swirling in unison and cutting the chilly morning air! Helicopters! The ground shook and the drone of engines grew, causing strong vibrations in my chest. Then, with a roar and a thunder, they flew straight over our yard, 20 metres high, almost clipping the tall swaying bamboo. They flew so close that we could see the white faces of the Rhodesian Special Forces Commandos painted black, sitting side-by-side, clutching their machine guns, facing out with their legs hanging over the sides of the open doors of the Rhodesian Air Force Alouette helicopters.

That picture, still as vivid as ever, is framed and etched in my mind. I stood there gaping, frozen, as those machines, three, four of them, flew, howling in the distance, dropping leaflets overboard. It was just like the movies. Then, almost as quickly as they had appeared, they were gone within seconds, their engines and rotors causing not more than a din in the distance as they flew South towards the border between Rhodesia and Zambia.

That characterised a period of heightened tension and conflict in the Frontline States at the time and, specifically, Zambia. Havoc and destabilisation reigned in those countries as the liberation movements, ZAPU, ZANU, SWAPO, and the ANC were targeted and internal pressure was applied to the racist regimes of Rhodesia and South Africa, militarily and by way of popular uprising. They retaliated. What is described above was a frequent occurrence as the racist Rhodesian and South African regimes used their militaries to terrorise liberation movement bases and leaders in the Frontline States. Numerous raids had been carried out in the sovereign territories of Mozambique, Lesotho, and Zambia with devastating and deadly consequences for local residents and liberation movement cadres. A full-scale conventional war waged as the SADF invaded Angola in an attempt by the apartheid SA regime to install a puppet regime and topple the MPLA-led government. Thousands of Angolan civilians perished as a result of that aggressive posture, prompting the Cubans to come to the aid of the Angolan Military FAPLA Armed Forces to repel the SADF.

Zambia, a refuge and base for liberation movements, had become a target. Danger lurked in Lusaka too during that period, as the Rhodesians, backed by the SADF, conducted late night and early morning raids into the country, targeting liberation movement safe houses and strategic infrastructure. On that fateful morning, we were to learn that the helicopters we saw had just attacked and bombed a ZAPU residence housing intelligence operatives. In the process of those raids, invariably, innocent civilians lost their lives in the crossfire. The raids intensified on bases and houses leading up to the 1980s. Hospitals filled up rapidly with victims of those raids and bloodstained sheets and overcrowded morgues became the norm rather than the exception. Ironically, the message in the pamphlets dropped by the helicopters read:

We are sorry, Zambians, for the inconvenience caused to you, but we have to fight with terrorists that are living among you and who your government is allowing to live in your country.

The Aviation Training Academy
O.R. Tambo Auditorium
was officially opened by
His Excellency
President Jacob Zuma
on 19 October 2017

Just like other liberation movements, the ANC, and particularly its leadership, had also become a target of the racist regime in Lusaka. In spite of all the terror and destruction that seized the Zambian capital city as the raids intensified, one resultant action was that it brought Uncle O. R. into more frequent and direct contact.

Although we had seen the leader, from a distance at ANC gatherings and events, we'd never been in close proximity to him. The heightened security situation meant that it was no longer safe for leaders of liberation movements to stay in one place. So, Uncle O. R.'s residence was no longer safe, and he had to be rotated between various houses when he was in town. The profile of those houses had to be low-key and not easily identified as ANC residences. My father was working with the UN at the time and, though involved in ANC activities, was not easily identified with the ANC. Our house fit the profile the ANC sought to secure Uncle O. R. and became one of the houses his security detail would use from time to time when he was in Lusaka.

I looked forward to Uncle O. R.'s visits as, for me, then a 10-year-old, they were preceded by serious drama, protocol and activity. His movements were not openly discussed or known to those whose houses he used. The first indications of his pending arrival would be an ANC vehicle hooting at the gate, which broke through the boredom as I struggled with my homework in the afternoon. That would be the security detail coming to check the house and I guess to quietly do what was necessary to secure the premises. For me, that meant running around the yard with the dogs in tow and following the security men as they inspected the property. The yard was not expansive, and the house small and modest, very basic with no elaborate external structures. It was similar to a typical South African township house. Internally, there was a communal bathroom (no shower), three simple rooms, a basic kitchen, and a combined dining room/living room, all with cement floors. Outside, there was a small yard and a gravel driveway. It was all so unassuming, which was one of the attributes that attracted Uncle O. R.'s security detail, apart from the fact that my father was known and trusted in ANC circles and the community in Zambia. It was exhilarating running with the dogs and following the security as they checked exit and entry points in the yard, probably to assess escape routes and potential entry points that might be used by sinister elements that needed to be watched and monitored while O. R. was around.

The build-up to his arrival was equally fascinating for me as he normally arrived in the evening. If I managed to stay awake, sustained by the excitement, I would be part of the family reception committee, dressed in my pyjamas and gown. When his small motorcade of Volvos entered the yard on the gravel road, we would be waiting on the verandah. Then, among his aides and security personnel, the diminutive but upright frame of Uncle O. R. would emerge, ever so gentle in demeanor and smiling, and he would come to greet and embrace us as he entered the house, just like a long-lost uncle coming to visit. Those were trying but exciting times for me. I will now continue this submission by way of a letter to the legendary Uncle O. R.:

Dear Uncle O. R.,

This may seem insensitive, but were it not for the Rhodesian raids into Zambia, I may have not have known you in the way I did. I recall with sharp clarity your working and official visits to Zambia when you would stay with us in Northmead in Lusaka. Until then, I had only known of you from the perspective of the ANC Pioneer Movement where we learned about the ANC, it historic mission, its values and leadership. We recited poems with your name and sang about you and other leaders of the ANC of that time in our activities.

When I met you face-to-face during your numerous visits to Lusaka, I connected to you from that early perspective, but I also just experienced you as a warm uncle whose humility and genuine compassion made you so approachable and easy to engage – even for me at a young age, when I didn't have much on which to engage with you at the time. My father's description of you sums that up very well: 'His easy and informal nature put one at ease and made one feel comfortable; there was no pretense about him and he was passionate about the people he engaged with.'

Whenever you visited, you fit into our humble little household and became part of the family. My mother remembers your sincerity when you interacted with people. I also witnessed that whenever you visited. Apart from the elaborate catering that became associated with your presence – full breakfasts with eggs and bacon and elaborate dinners with a variety of meat – the affinity people had for you lingers as a memory until today. Our house would become a meeting point where people would come to consult with you: the comrades, colleagues, officials and friends would constantly come in and go out, and you had time for all of them.

At an older age, as I became more conscious politically, following your writings and listening to you on the radio and in interviews and documentaries, and I began to understand you more intimately politically and as a person. The genuineness witnessed when you were at our home translated to the way you conducted yourself in the public domain. You spoke with conviction and passion about the plight of the suffering masses under the yoke of colonialism and apartheid – almost as if you carried their pain – and you conveyed it in your warm and gentle manner, which is why you were revered at home, in the Frontline States, throughout the continent of Africa and on the global stage by world leaders across the geopolitical divide at the time.

Your humility and ability to adapt at a personal level and connect with us as a family in our very basic setting reflected the way you came across in public as you engaged to expose the criminality of the apartheid system. Through the humility you displayed among your comrades, not only did you lead them, you lived among them. The story is told by one of the MK operatives, now a veteran, of how you lived in a safe house with them in Makeni, a residential area in Lusaka, sharing communal sleeping areas and taking part in the chores of the house, such as cleaning and cooking. You had no airs about yourself and, as the leader of the ANC, you had no expectations of special privileges or the need to be worshipped by your followers: rather, you got involved and integrated yourself into people's lives. You understood the context at the time – hard and trying times, as my father puts it, for the ANC community,

not only in Zambia but throughout the region, the Frontline States, and especially in South Africa. You could have chosen to stay in hotels, which would have fit with your stature and rank. You could have stayed with your ally and gracious host, Kenneth Kaunda, at a guesthouse on Zambia's State House premises like your counterpart, ZAPU leader Joshua Nkomo, did after his house was bombed by the Rhodesians and he narrowly escaped death in Lusaka. But you opted to live among us, the people, as you had always done, as if to encourage, assure and demonstrate that you were with us.

And yet, you could be direct and frank with those you engaged with, still in an ever-articulate and gentle manner. I still enjoy watching you in documentaries telling Western media why the ANC adopted a policy of engaging and soliciting help, material and financial, from Eastern Bloc communist countries aligned to the Soviet Union. And you did so without any apprehension. You asked slowly and deliberately, 'What does it matter? What does it matter that we are assisted by those countries?', reminding them that those were countries committed to assisting the ANC with defeating the evil and immoral apartheid system in South Africa and who had responded to the liberation movements' call for assistance. When it came to the ANC policy shift to the MK targeting soft targets inside of South Africa, you did not mince your words and stated that the ANC's hand had been forced into that policy change, and you pointed to the death and destruction waged by the racist apartheid regime against innocent citizens in South Africa and those of our allies in the Frontline states, Zambia being no exception. Your selflessness as a leader is sorely missed today. Your mission was fulfilling the mandate thrust upon you by your comrades on the eve of the banning of the ANC: to take the struggle of emancipation from oppression in South Africa to the global political stage and sustain the ANC in exile. You left the country with nothing but a suitcase and the clothes on your back; you had no resources or infrastructure; you had nothing. Through sheer resolve, discipline and determination, you built the ANC with your abilities and your leadership team into a formidable force outside of South Africa. You did that with your superior interpersonal and relationship-building skills, which I witnessed as a child, and your ability to engage and connect as you criss-crossed continents, networking with various structures, formations and leaders. Your ability to mobilise and motivate the leadership of the ANC – internally and externally – to deliver on that mandate is also testament to how you steered the ANC: through others, as clearly you could not have achieved all that you did singlehandedly, which you understood.

You achieved all of that selflessly and with a steadfast commitment to the mission of the ANC. You did not seek personal glory or ask to be hero-worshipped. Instead, you motivated your leadership to galvanise the world to support the cause of the ANC and the plight of the suffering Black majority peoples of South Africa. You put the plight of the ANC's leadership – who were incarcerated on Robben Island – at the forefront. You built the image and stature of your friend and comrade, Nelson Mandela, in the eyes of the international community and created a brand around him and his name, eventually propelling him to the leadership of the ANC and the country as the first democratically elected president of South Africa in a post-apartheid dispensation. You could have chosen to put yourself forward and branded the organisation around you: instead, you displayed a selfless style of leadership seldom seen in South Africa or globally.

All of your acts and achievements in fulfilling your mandate to guide the ANC and locate it internationally were due to your passion for the people of South Africa and the cause of their freedom, not because you were driven by self gratification or reward. That same passion you displayed to us as a family and the numerous other families and people you interacted with, and in turn, your exemplary behavior and value system, moved people to emulate you and work tirelessly and muster the courage and resilience to fight the evil apartheid system in South Africa and on the global stage.

Uncle O. R., we sorely miss you, and, as we celebrate your centenary this year of 2017, we reflect on your life when you were in our midst. We celebrate your tireless efforts and committed discipline in fostering solidarity with the progressive peoples of the African continent and the international stage, forging partnerships that would eventually overthrow the racist apartheid government in South Africa. We reflect on your tireless efforts that led to the adoption of the historic Harare Declaration, the midwife of the multiparty Codesa negotiations that led to a free and democratic South Africa in 1994, led by your friend, Comrade President Nelson Mandela.

What an end to a beautiful chapter choreographed and directed by you. As we grapple with the challenges of leading the national democratic revolution in the second chapter, I cannot help but reflect and remember you. As I observe the current context in South Africa's political, civil service, private, civil society, and labour sectors, and all of the accompanying leadership and governance challenges we are confronted with, I cannot help but reflect on you and contend that you were one-of-a-kind, a messiah, a towering giant.

How I wish that we would all stop at this critical juncture in South Africa's history: a point at which we have lost our way as the ANC and our position as leaders of our society. We must reflect on your authentic and ethical transformational leadership and what you achieved during your time as leader of the ANC (amid numerous challenges). How I wish we could emulate you and lead from your purview and reference in South Africa and Africa today.

Continue resting in peace Uncle O. R., former Comrade President of the African National Congress. We miss you during this difficult period.

Dumisani Sangweni

Memory of Uncle O. R. Tambo

It was late at night, and I was in a deep sleep when, suddenly, my slumber was disturbed by my mother shaking me gently. 'Lindi, wake up. Wake up.' And then a little louder because I was not responding, 'Lindiwe, *vuka*, wake up. We have a visitor.'

I woke up, a little confused, and not understanding what visitor had arrived in the thick of the night. The lights in my bedroom were turned on by my mother. I could hear voices in the living room. My father's voice was distinct, and other voices I did not recognise.

I was awake then, and my mind was racing.

'What's going on?' I asked my mother.

She explained that we had unexpected visitors. An uncle had arrived and, therefore, I had to give up my room so he could be accommodated there. I walked drowsily to my parents room, where my brother Dumisani was already curled up in the middle of their bed. My mother had made up the rollaway bed, and so I climbed onto it and fell asleep immediately, as the voices from the living room of the unnamed visitors and my father continued in deep conversation, late into the night.

The next day arrived, and it was a school day, so my younger brother and I went about our routine of getting ready. His bedroom and mine were closed, and behind the doors were the sleeping visitors. We were both wide awake then and extremely curious as our mother supervised our dressing up. During the night, she had had the presence of mind to take our school clothes out so we could dress in the morning.

'Who arrived last night?' Dumi asked, bursting with curiosity. Our mother responded, 'Uncle O. R. Tambo.'

We were mesmerised, as we knew who he was: the president of the ANC!

'What? How come?' We asked at the same time.

So our mother explained that Uncle O. R. was brought, late at night, by his bodyguards and driver to spend the night at our house. Years later, we understood better: our house was a safe house that had been cleared by ANC President O. R. Tambo to be used as a place of safety when the need arose. They had not felt safe that night, so he had been relocated to our house, which happened a few more times.

By the time we got to breakfast, my mother had set the dining room table with her best tablecloth: a damask one with strawberry applique. The frying pan was sizzling with lovely little brown sausages and onions. Ours was a very important visitor, as that type of fare was only served on special days or the occasional Sunday as a treat.

As we finished our breakfast, our father announced that it was time to leave, and the door leading from the passage suddenly opened and out stepped the most impeccably dressed man. It really was him: ANC President O. R. Tambo.
'Good morning!' he greeted us warmly. Our mother introduced us: 'This is Lindiwe.'

His open arms received me, and he drew me spontaneously into a big bear hug. 'And this is our son, Dumisani!' He also received an affectionate hug.

What a nice uncle is all we could talk about as our father drove us to school.

Dear Uncle O. R.,

That was my first up-close-and-personal encounter with you. You were a giant in my young mind and, even now, at the age of 50, you remain a giant in my memories. I was born in Swaziland, in 1966, to parents who traversed the world from Swaziland to Holland to Zambia. In 1974, my parents became active in the ANC, given that the home of the African National Congress was in Lusaka, Zambia.

Following my first real encounter with you, my next encounter would be at Aunty Rita Mfenyana's home in Lusaka where, every Saturday, she ran a youth club, the ANC Masupatsela – some of us were a little younger than the official youth age. There were littler ones too, like Sisonke Msimang and Ndlela Nkobi, who were still toddlers. We were taught the Freedom Charter and could recite it verbatim:

> We, the People of South Africa, declare for all our country and the world to know that: South Africa belongs to all who live in it, Black and white, and that no government can justly claim authority unless it is based on the will of all the people.

We broke into song, so well-prepared for the occasion when you would visit us, talk to us and motivate us.

'Tambo uyingwe! Uyingwe!'

'Wen' uyingwe!'

And then we did the gumboot dance, and then poetry, followed by *indlamu*. I still remember how proud you looked as you watched our performance in the audience of parents who watched alongside you, content that your children would one day be citizens of their free South Africa; where the playing fields would be evened out by the sweat and blood of our fathers and mothers, and later our brothers and sisters: the youth of 1976.

Lindiwe Sangweni-Siddo

Fast-forward to 8 September 1986. It was six months after Prime Minister Olof Palme's assassination. The weather was a typical autumn day, and the leaves had begun to turn into hues of red, burnt orange and yellow, some already falling on the ground. My feet crunched some of the dried crispy leaves as I walked briskly to catch the train that would take me from the suburb of Kista to the Stockholm city centre, the cool air accosting my nostrils and my hands digging into my pockets for warmth. I missed the hot and sunny weather of Nairobi and wished I was back home.

My Aunt Lindiwe was the Chief Representative of the African National Congress for all of the Scandinavian countries and she was based in Stockholm, Sweden. She had arranged for me to join her for a six-month stint of politicisation, working alongside her and other ANC comrades in the office of the African National Congress. I had just completed a Pittman secretarial course under the tutelage of my mother at the Valley Secretarial College in Nairobi, Kenya, so my newfound skills were proving to be useful as I was given assignments by my aunt and other Comrades in the office to type various documents, speeches, press releases and my aunt's poetry.

I finally made it to the office and cast a cursory glance over my shoulders, left and then right to check if I was being followed.

That was standard security practice we had been shown by Comrade Jerry Matsila who reminded us that even though we were far from South Africa, the apartheid regime had its moles planted all over the world to sabotage the work of the ANC. So security measures were second nature to us. The entrance to the office was off a main street and down an alley. It was not a prominent address: in fact, it reminded a lot of the alley that led to the ANC headquarters in Lusaka, Zambia.

I unlocked the main door, pushed it inwards and let myself in, ensuring that the door was closed behind me. I then rode up in the old lift and it let me out on the third floor. Once on that level, I had to unlock another solid steel door and then climb the stairs to the fourth floor of an attic-like office. I knocked and Comrade Mohamed let me in.

It was a typical Monday with piles of documents waiting me to be typed and checked by the Chief, Aunty Lindiwe, and Comrades Mohamed and Jerry. So I set about my work and later heard that my Aunt had arrived.

'Lindana!' she called to me from her office. '*Unjani mntaka Bhuti*?' she greeted me, with loving warm eyes, and caressed my hands as I stood at her desk smiling back and greeting her. She had strict

instructions to follow a different routine from all of us, so her arrival times at the office varied, as did her mode of transport to the office. We never really asked how she got there. She would just arrive and be there.

'I have an assignment for you, Sthandwa,' she continued in her honey-like, creamy voice. 'Please can you book a call for me to speak to my counterpart in Nigeria at 2 p.m. this afternoon? I will be with Uncle Caiphus Semenya this morning; we have a meeting in the Old Town of Stockholm. We'll be back in time for the call.'

International calls were still booked in those days – we could not dial international numbers directly – they had to be booked by calling an international operator who then booked the call at the requested time, and then, at exactly the time you requested, the international operator would get back to you to transfer your call.

So I went about executing that request and arranged for the ANC Chief Representative located in Nigeria to receive a call from Comrade Lindiwe Mabuza. Once done: back to my work of typing and meeting the various deadlines.

My aunt left and only Comrade Mohamed and I were left in the office. At about 1.30 p.m. a telephone call came through, and friend from Peru came to see Comrade Mohamed. I decided to make coffee for all of us. I passed the office that they were sitting in, a small reception office facing the door that led from the stairwell, and proceeded to the meeting room. The kettle was located in that room, so I turned it on and prepared the cups, milk and sugar for our coffees.

Suddenly, from nowhere, came the loudest explosion I have ever heard. BOOOOOM!! My fight or flight reaction was to dive under the boardroom table – probably a security measure I had heard somewhere and parked in my subconscious mind. Had the kettle exploded? My mind was racing. The room was filling up with smoky putrid fumes. I started coughing and crawled out from under the table. With my arms stretched out in front of me so I would not bump into anything, I made my way back to the reception office, where I could hear Comrade Mohamed and the other gentleman also coughing and spluttering.

'Lindi!' Comrade Mohamed called out my name. I could hear the panic in his voice.

The fumes were growing stronger.

'We've been bombed!' he shouted. I made it into the office as he pushed the attic window open to let in some air. We moved to the window and took turns to breathe in the air from outside. The thick, white fumes had engulfed the entire office. We could not see anything.

My heart pumped and my mind raced. Was this the end? Where was Aunty Lindiwe? Had they killed her? I held back the tears. That was not a time to cry.

We heard sirens wailing below us, first in the distance and then downstairs. Help was on its way. Soon voices could be heard as the firefighters made their way to the office. We were evacuated and I still remember how we stepped through a pile of concrete dust where once the solid steel door had been. Now, it was crumpled like tin foil that had been crushed by a giant hand. The solid cement that had kept foes out of bounds was no more: it had been blown apart. That was the door my Aunty Lindiwe would have been opening a few minutes before 2 p.m. had she been in time for the international call I had booked for her earlier that day.

The three of us were led down the stairs – many flights – to get to the ground floor where ambulances and police cars were lined up. The news of the incident was in all of the papers that evening and the next day.

Over 40 years later, I am now a grown woman, living in a free South Africa. I am the owner of the Soweto Hotel and Conference Centre located at the Walter Sisulu Square of Dedication – or Freedom Square, as it is known colloquially. That is where our Freedom Charter was adopted on 26 June 1955. We still have a long way to go to achieve the freedom we declared so assuredly in our youth. Today, the youth of South Africa are looking up to us, their elders, for the same guidance we looked for when we encountered you in our youth.

Uncle O. R., I think if you were still alive, you would say:

The real struggle for freedom has only just begun. We softened the battlefield with our blood, tears and sweat; it is now up to you, the next generation, to show leadership and take charge. No South African, Black or white, should rest until you, the people of South Africa, pledge to strive together, sparing neither strength nor courage, until the democratic changes set out in our Freedom Charter have been won for all South Africans.

Lindiwe Sangweni-Siddo

Monday, 8 September 1986

A bomb exploded in the office of the ANC on the third floor of an office block in Stockholm, Sweden. The office was severely damaged but nobody was killed despite the presence of three people. Among the survivors ed was the ANC's representative in Sweden, Lindiwe Mabuza.

My Aunty Lindiwe survived by the grace of God. Her meeting with Caiphus Semenya had taken longer than expected, so their return to the ANC office was delayed. The timing of the explosion coincided with the international call booked for 2 p.m. that afternoon.

The bombing was part of the apartheid government's strategy in the 1970s and 80s to eliminate or neutralise South African liberation movements outside of the country: the ANC office in London was bombed in March 1982; in September 1986, the ANC office in Stockholm, Sweden was bombed, and in March 1988, the ANC's Chief Representative in France, Dulcie September, was shot and killed in Paris. www.sahistory.org.za/dated-event/diplomatic-office-anc-Stockholm-bombed.

Dear Uncle O. R.,

As we mark your 100th birthday, I remember our enthusiasm in the ANC Youth League as we organised a rally in honour of your 75th birthday, which was our first rally as the leadership structure of the ANC Youth Section and the South African Youth Congress (Sayco) with Peter Mokaba as chairperson and I as the deputy. At that rally, we declared you the Honorary Life President of the ANC Youth League.

Born in Johannesburg in 1958, I was blessed to have been moulded by you and other great leaders of our country.

I cannot remember when I first met you, but it was in Morogoro where my sister Thaninga and I made tea for you and other uncles and aunties.

Since then, you have been present at all of the important milestones of my life: when I chose my career, when I got married, when Thaninga got married, and when my brother Lenin and Nosithembele named their first born, Oliver Shope, after you.

I remember the day in Lusaka when you whispered for a piece of oxtail, which you were not allowed to eat, and when Mom found out, we were all in deep trouble.

I also recall our wedding day with Tebogo Mafole when you were outraged at the sweet and sour pork cooked by comrade Mavis (Thandi Ndlovu) and her team. You kept asking who had poured sugar into the pork. But I was also mad that you wore a shirt made from material donated by the Scandinavians, which Comrades used to make everything under the sun: tablecloths, sheets, dresses, etc. Those are special memories.

Your prioritising education impacted me significantly. I remember how many young Comrades were upset that you insisted that their first responsibility to South Africa, before MK, was going to school. During our university days in Cuba, we felt less revolutionary because we could not, like our comrades from the Palestinian Liberation Organisation, go for military training during the holidays. Today, I appreciate your wisdom and vision.

In 1978, the World Youth Festival, organised by the World Federation of Democratic Youth (WFDY), was held in Havana Cuba and you were given special recognition by President Fidel Castro. The ANC Youth Section, led by comrade Eddie Funde, had a big delegation and was honoured to give the closing speech.

It was in Havana that you advised me to study telecommunications engineering because few women did that.

I was not surprised because it was under your leadership that Mom was appointed Chief Representative of the ANC in Lusaka, and I had also heard that you had insisted that Sis Lindiwe Mabuza was more than equal to the task of representing the in the Nordic countries, an honour that touched her deeply. Thank you for your consistency in supporting women.

I so miss your principled leadership and the ANC I grew up in whose values I committed to uphold when I left to join the team that co-founded the Congress of the People under the leadership of comrade Mosiuoa Lekota.

Lyndall Shope Mafole

Wedding of Tebogo Mafole and Lyndall Shope.
L to R: Gertrude Shope, (the late) Tebogo Mafole, Lyndall, Uncle Maroo and Uncle O. R.

Dear O. R.,

This letter is long overdue. Thank you for taking the time to talk to me many years ago in what would become one of the most defining conversations of my life. We had a chance meeting in mid-1992 in the elevator of Shell House when you recognised me immediately, even though we hadn't seen each other since my childhood gumboot-dancing days. I very enthusiastically accepted your invitation to visit your office.

That was the first time I had seen you since your stroke. I was taken aback by the toll of the stroke on your hands, your speech, and your movements. I still had childhood images of your strong stride and decisive way of talking. In spite of the stroke, you were still able to fill a room with your presence.

You asked me about my next steps in life, as I had just graduated from high school. I told you that I felt stuck because almost all of the 'grown-ups' (except for my mother) were telling me to abandon my dream of making films and to pursue something more 'practical and useful'. You asked me why I wanted to be a filmmaker. I told you that all of the career dreams I had had up to that point were because of seeing those professions so brilliantly portrayed on TV and in film. I, too, wanted to tell stories with that kind of impact, even if they were told on a smaller scale. You thought about my answer for a while. Then, as expected, you told

me that my father and the other naysayers were speaking from a place of love and concern. They wanted to ensure that I fulfilled my potential and would be able to take care of myself.

You then turned the conversation in a most unexpected direction. You said that, even though I should consider their feedback, at the end of the day, I was responsible for my own decisions. On my deathbed, I alone would be accountable for my choices, and I would have no one else to blame for those decisions. I had to make my own decisions. Most importantly, though, whatever I ended up doing, I should always strive to be the best I could be.

What must have been a passing conversation for you changed how I moved through this thing called life. At 18, I was asked to think about all of my choices through the lens of my mortality. That conversation impacted many of my future decisions, including what I work on, and whom and how I love. It is when I forget your words that I lose my way.

I shared this story on stage a few years ago in Brooklyn, New York, and I realised that, even though I think about you often, I don't talk about you enough. I believe everyone should know about you.

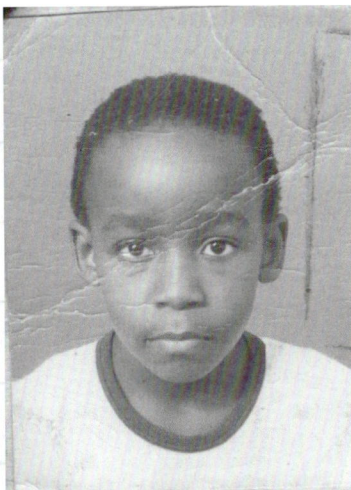

Thank you for your leadership, wisdom, empathy and time. I am forever grateful.

Love,

Ndlela Nkobi

My Dear President,

While I don't remember the first day I met you (toddlers should remember being cradled by a man such as you... I am sorry I do not!), I carry with me fond memories of you. There was the look of horror on your face when mum served you a whole fish, head and tail, on one of those rare occasions when you joined us for lunch in our small home in Lusaka, Zambia (I know you forgave her. As a French woman married to a Zulu man from Alexandra, you saw how quickly she got to grips with the varied pallets of South Africans, and learned to master both prawn tandoori and mogodu — even clearing it straight from the slaughter!). There were also your surrepticious visits to our flat, in and out like a flash, whispering to Baba whatever you needed him to know or do before you hugged me warmly, smiled, and left.

We didn't see much of you in those days. Or ever for that matter. I had an idea of how taxing your life could be. Between Baba's travelling where he was the NEC member responsible for international affairs to his discretion and secrecy as secretary of the Political Military Council, I remember him being away a lot during the 80s. It must have been much worse for you and your family. But somehow you never lost your warmth...

It has been a while since I last saw you. I have news: I finally became a lawyer! After all those years of dreaming of it, it is now a reality. Thank you for the encouragement. For not laughing at my 8-year-old self when I said this is what I wanted to do. Most adults, hearing that from a child that age, would have dismissed it as a flight of fancy. You did not. You took me seriously. You said I should go for it. You said it would be hard work but I would love it. You were right. Besides being able to help others in more ways than I had imagined, as you predicted, it is also a constructive way of channelling my argumentative side...

I grew up knowing you were my President, and it took a while to be able to think of anyone else as such... I am grateful for it. It made me think of leaders as humble hard-working self-effacing men and women whose commitment to a cause never falters.

We still need such leaders today, that's for sure. Economic hardship for most of your people, and inequality of access to resources, has made tensions we saw dissipate during our transition, tensions the reconciliation process was meant to address, rise considerably. We're not yet the rainbow nation we were meant to become. It doesn't help that few have either the

inclination or the gravitas to push for the realisation of your dream South Africa.

I live with that tension every day. I am still considered weird and odd here. 'What kind of coloured has a name like Nokukhanya Jele?' And here am I, never having thought of myself as a 'coloured'. Not being able to fit into the label given to me in a society that knows only labels. Not being understood, even in today's South Africa, when I answer questions of 'where did you get that first name?' with the truth: 'my father chose it'; when I describe myself as a "first generation mixture" or as my maternal grandmother lovingly called me, as "pain d'épices" (literally 'gingerbread' in English). If I mention I was born in Helsinki, Finland, it simply aggravates the confusion. I am endlessly flabbergasted at how a country with such diversity still cannot fathom its people mixing, making children together, having multicultural upbringings. This in a place where descendants of Dutch settlers speak flawless isiZulu or Sesotho, where peoples come from all corners of the world and have for centuries. My own daily battle with the 'what kind of human are you?' questions pale in comparison to the xenophobia that plagues our streets. How did a people who owe so much to the generosity of others when their own were refugees, stoop to so badly treating the descendants of those who sheltered, fed, and welcomed them?

I know it would pain you to see this.

But let me not be despondent. That would serve no purpose. The mere act of writing to you reminds me I have no excuse but to remain committed to doing what I can to help change things for the better. After all, where would we be if you had thrown your hands in the air and given up?! I won't. I promise.

Comradely yours, my President.
With love,
Nolukhanya

Dear Comrade President O. R.,

Mr Oliver Reginald Tambo
President of the African National Congress
ANC Headquarters
Lusaka, Zambia

Ref.: Greetings from the Administrative Coordinator of the ANC
Development Centre – Dakawa, Morogoro

This is Mary Ngozi, Administrative Coordinator for the ANC
Development Centre in Dakawa, Morogoro. I was appointed by
the ANC Mazimbu-Dakawa Directorate headed by Comrade Tikley
Mohammed in 1983.

Comrade President, I hope you will still remember that Uncle
Dennis, Somafco Project Manager and Comrade Tim Maseko,
Somafco Principal, were also members of the Directorate who
were responsible for ensuring that Mazimbu and Dakawa
were properly administered and managed as they were being
developed. They were all appointed by the NEC.

Comrade President, I have the pleasure of writing this letter
to you to convey my warmest congratulations to you on your
100th anniversary this year of 2017. I do not have much to give
you except my deepest love and respect for the encouragement
and attention you accorded to me while visiting the ANC
Development Centre in Dakawa-Morogoro in 1984.

I remember your visit vividly like it was yesterday because I
was so nervous and sweating when I was informed by Uncle
Oswald Dennis that I was to present the floor plans to you for
the development of Dakawa. I want to believe that Comrade
President O. R. remembers and knows Uncle Dennis very well. He
was appointed by the National Executive Committee of the ANC
to build the Solomon Mahlangu Freedom College (Somafco) in
Mazimbu, Morogoro after the 1976 SOWETO uprisings.

Comrade President, you listened very carefully while noticing my
anxiety to do right and not make any mistakes: I was very nervous
as I was meeting you for the first time – so close – except for your
visit to the camps in Angola.

Comrade President, O. R., you held my hand warmly and looked
at me and smiled. From that moment on, my fears were blown
out the window as I galloped with the architectural plans given
to me by Uncle Dennis and Comrade Spenser Hodgson, the ANC
Mazimbu and Dakawa Architect. It took me about 30 minutes
to present those to you and your accompanying delegation as I
offered to answer questions during the presentation.

Her Excellence N. M. Sibande Thusi presenting her credentials to Russian President Vlad Putin

When I finished, you looked at me and said ,'How proud the ANC is for having you at this very young age (I had told the President during introduction of all staff members at the centre earlier on that I was 25 when I was appointed the administrative coordinator of Dakawa) doing such difficult and demanding work.' An you continued, ' We all know of the difficult conditions you live under as many of our young people cross the storm created by the apartheid regime and travel from parts our country seeking refuge in the ANC. We are proud of all of you in Mazimbu and Dakawa for the work you do and the sacrifices you are making in order to liberate our people from the bondage of the apartheid regime.'

Comrade President O. R., you shook our hands warmly one by one and told the team and Comrades to support me in all we do for the comfort of the ANC community in the Development Centre and that we should work collectively as we do because teamwork is the mother of victory.

Thereafter, we accompanied you around the important parts of the Centre, where you met students who were in classes studying under trees, and they were enthusiastic and working hard in order to meet the admission criteria for acceptance at the Solomon Mahlangu Freedom College (Somafco) while others were

Adults: Tiny Nokwe, wife of first African advocate; Duma Nokwe, mother of Nosizwe Nokwe and grandmother of Vuyo Skweyiya (both contributors); Catherine Jele, mother of Nokukhanya Jele (contributor); Rita Mfenyana : manager of Masupatsela in Lusaka
Children: Left to right, Mandlesilo Msimang (Sisonke's sibling), Nokukhanya Jele, Sisonke Msimang, Dumisani Sangweni (last three all contributors).

preparing for scholarships abroad. You expressed satisfaction with everything you had seen and said, 'We are very humbled with your reception and very proud of you all for all the work you do for our people. Keep it up.'

I am very happy, Comrade President, that yes, we keep on going and doing our best to serve the movement and our people. Today, Somafco and the ANC Development Centre in Dakawa are icons of remembrance to the Tanzanian people, which confirms the historical relationship between the peoples of both countries.

Finally, I am happy to report, Comrade President, that, thanks to the African National Congress (ANC), I have since acquired additional knowledge and experience and continue to serve in the diplomatic service of the Republic of South Africa.

My continued strength, courage, commitment and confidence was deepened on that day in 1984 when you, Comrade President O. R., with your warm, soft hand touched mine when I was presenting the ANC Development Centre plans to you. Today, I am privileged to represent the Republic of South Africa at the Russian Federation.

Comrade President, I wish to end with my best wishes to you and your family as I wish you a very happy 100th anniversary this year. Please pass my regards to Aunt Adelaide.

Most sincerely

(Mary Ngozi)

Nomasonto Maria Sibanda-Thusi
Ambassador

Our Dearest Uncle O. R.,

Why did you have to go? Why, before 1994, having given your all to the struggle ...

We are the children of Mary and Au-Rheims Gaobepe. Soga, our older brother, was born on 3 February 1950 in Taung, South Africa; I, Nomsa, was born on 25 December 1953 in Kimberly, South Africa, and Neo, our last born, was came into this world on 27 April 1959 (South Africa's Freedom Day) in Kitwe, Northern Rhodesia.

Our family left South Africa in 1958 for Northern Rhodesia to escape Bantu education. Eventually, we settled in the city of Lusaka, and that is when you, Uncle, came to live with us at number 1 Chitemwiko Close, Kabulonga, at Ruth Mompati's (our father's cousin) recommendation, she having known our roots and family lifestyle.

Iyooooo, Uncle, it was having you in our simple Kabulonga home that gave us the opportunity to encounter the likes of Duma Nokwe, Thabo Mbeki, Thomas Nkobi, Chris Hani, Jacob Zuma, Pallo Jordan, Joe Modise, Sindiso Mfenyane, Jimmy Stewart, the Steve Tshwetes, the list is endless. We never thought that South Africa would be free in our lifetime. We thought that might happen only in our great grandchildrens' time.

You had foresight and fortitude, and you carried yourself with such dignity and pride. We were in awe of you. Ironically, you also look like our Dad, as if you were brothers.

Are you still humble, like when on occasion you'd grace our kitchen and make yourself a cup of tea? You went further and made a big production one Christmas and roasted a turkey with potatoes and we were like: 'What? Uncle? Today!' What memories!

Do you remember telling our mother, 'Sis Mary, your kitchen is so clean, it's as if you never use it!' We, the girls, have taken after her.

Odd or whatever, we Gaobepe children never spoke much of your family or of politics with you; we guessed, as children, that you discussed enough of that with your peers and we didn't want to see you hurting.

We proudly recall you asking Nomsa how her trip to South Africa (Transkei) was and her replying that the consumer boycotts were successful, and you beamed happily.

We wondered whether you were aware that our mum often used her business trips, as requested by the ANC, to secretly carry letters to and from South Africa.

That was Nomsa's experience – with Neo. On two occasions, she was telephoned and told not to come home until morning. Imagine that, at a party!

Neo thanked you for gracing her wedding to Ike Nzo. Then, there is the infamous picture where you have your finger in his ear to make sure that it was clean. Later on, Neo and Ike delighted having you for Sunday lunches at Chainama Hills Hospital where there was to be strictly no salt at all in your food.

We thank you for visiting mum at the Johannesburg Hospital when she had her triple bypass, walking those long corridors after having your stroke in Europe.

Neo, too, thanks you for visiting her in hospital with Aunty Adelaide when she was sick.

Looking back, Uncle, there were times, as children, when our home and family were targeted with threats of being bombed by the boers, and it was very emotional and difficult for us.

Imagine coming home from a party and finding a note on our infamous big black gate saying, 'Go back to where you were, the boers are bombing.'

On a somber note, Soga had a stroke in December 2014. Sometimes, because of his condition, he proudly remembers sharing his room with you in Lusaka, Zambia. You are his hero. To date, he has a big framed poster of you in his room. You told him then, 'Soga, with hard work, anything is possible.' And you were right.

Today, through your hard work, South Africa has realised its freedom.

Uncle, there is a portrait of yours that is very popular now in South Africa. In it, you are wearing a yellow embroidered African shirt that was made by our mother at her boutique in Lusaka, Zambia. We look at it with pride and joy whenever we see it.

By the way, we sold our Kalulanga home in Lusaka. It is now the Palestinian Embassy. (Neo worked at that embassy for some time.)

I wish you were here. We will tell you all when we meet. Lots happening.

All our love,

Soga, Nomsa and Neo Gaobepe XXX

Aluta continua ... the struggle continues.

Dearest Uncle O. R.,

My name is Norah Nolele Ntshona-Appolus. My mother was Putuse Leonora Appolus nee Dywili. She was from Cofimvaba in the Transkei, South Africa. She was married to my stepfather, Emil Appolus, a Namibian freedom fighter. Both of my parents were active in the Namibian liberation struggle with Swapo and we went into exile circa 1959.

I wonder if you remember when and where we first met? I don't: not because you were easily forgettable, not by any stretch of the imagination, but simply because I was so young at the time. That was in Dar es Salaam, in then Tanganyika, and it must easily have been circa 1963!

What I remember very clearly Uncle, was the beautiful red Irish linen party dress you brought me from London. Boy, that was one classy dress! It had smocking across the chest, a Peter Pan collar and a white cotton petticoat, so it flared slightly. I know it was Irish linen 'coz it said so on the hem in indelible black ink. I even had that dress on when I met President Julius Nyerere at State House (and I have a picture to prove it!) That was my favourite dress, and of course, you went up quite a few notches in my esteem and quickly and unequivocally became my 'favourite' uncle! Even when we moved to Zambia in 1965, I had that dress. Mum and I took some photos and, guess what? I was wearing

the dress! I wore that dress until it literally reached my navel, and then, one day, it mysteriously disappeared! Yeah, I guess Mum decided it was time to get rid of it but she could've asked me first!

I can't remember if I saw you in the intervening years when we lived in Lilanda, the go-to suburb for liberation movements in Lusaka, but of course I must have. I'm positive you must have come to our house for tea or something, especially when we moved to Olympia Park. If the truth be told, we were giggly teenagers then and, alas, not interested in the myriad uncles that regularly traipsed through our front door. Our undivided attention was captured by the young residents of the famous – or infamous – 'residence' in Lilanda and the merits of each resident who certainly had us in their thrall with their Duke of Argyll-patterned socks and pullovers and the ubiquitous white t-shirts!

Let's fast forward a decade or so when we're in Paris where I'm working for Radio France International's English Service 'Paris Calling Africa'.

Since I started working there, you, Uncle Johnny Makathini, and the other Comrades from the ANC and Swapo become regular interviewees. I remember that, one time, there was a United Nations conference on Africa in Paris. You naturally led the ANC delegation. Kingsley Makhabela was your bodyguard, and he had the room next to yours. Of course, I'd met Kingsley on my annual pilgrimage to Lusaka, so I knew him well. I naturally asked for an interview with you – an exclusive – and Kingsley agreed. It turned out that the interview only materialised the following day and my colleague and I had to camp in Kingsley's room the entire night. And there you were: a giant of a man, so gentle, so soft-spoken, so passionate about the freedom of your people. I was truly in awe and humbled to be in the presence of greatness and yet made to feel completely at ease. But then again, that was your trademark, wasn't it?

The next time I saw you was at Windhoek International Airport in independent Namibia when I was covering your state visit. You were accompanied by Dali and were en route to South Africa. That was the first time I saw you since your stroke. I broke down and cried as you made your way slowly but so dignified down the guard of honour. Dali took me in his arms but it was cold comfort.

The next time I saw you, which was also the last, was at that valiant son of the soil, Chris Hani's funeral in Johannesburg in April 1993, a fortuitous month as it turned out, for you were to join our ancestors later that month.

Photo was taken circa 1963 at State House in Dar es Salaam and there was a fete on the grounds of State House and I was taken by President Nyerere's daughter Anna (on the far left) to go and meet him. I'm the one on the right, holding the president's arm and I'm wearing the famous red linen dress gifted to me by Uncle O. R. on one of his visits to Dar. The little boy on the right is my brother Jomo.

I will always remember you: your greatness was not in the numerous speeches or words you spoke but in your humility and gentleness: a leader at the service of his people, imbued with an innate sense of justice and fairness.

Norah Nolele Appolus

Letter to O. R. Tambo: My years in the USSR

I did all of my schooling in Zambia because my parents, Vuyiswa and Duma Nokwe, were in exile from the early 1960s. I completed my secondary schooling in Lusaka at Kabulonga Girls'.

In those days, there was only one university in Lusaka, so competition for entry was extremely high and understandably, too, preference was given to Zambian citizens.

Nonetheless, we, the Masupatsela of the ANC already knew at that time that if we studied hard enough, we could be eligible for scholarships to the then socialist countries. I cannot purport to know how that practice came about, but I do know that it happened during Uncle O. R.'s time as the president of the ANC. It was a very comforting thought to know that, come what may, even though we were not in our own country, the organisation would ensure that we had access to tertiary education.

The moment arrived when we completed secondary school and left Lusaka for Mazimbu (Somafco), headed for different countries. When we left, we were not sure of our final destinations and were advised by the education department that we would be placed from Mazimbu.

After three months in Mazimbu, where we underwent intense political education about what it meant to be a cadre of the ANC, we were released to the world under strict instructions that we were now ambassadors of the movement and that we should always keep the flag of our glorious movement flying high.

We soon learnt that our being in the USSR on a scholarship was the result of our movement organising scholarships for ANC students through the Afro-Asian Solidarity Committee, which was a stroke of genius.

If I had to give you stories about the 10 years I spent there, we would have to write a new book. Suffice to say, those were the most interesting, exciting, enlightening, trying years of my life, but I emerged smiling, having graduated twice, first in 1984 with a diploma in chemical engineering in Baku (cum laude), and then in 1990 with my master's in petrochemical engineering in Moscow. Did I mention that we had to study in Russian? The first word we learnt was *tavarish* (comrade). I also earned myself a certificate as a Russian translator.

Imagine how we felt when we arrived in 1979 in Baku Azerbaijan, possibly the first country in the world where oil was processed into its different components. Under your leadership, the planning that our ANC education department must have gone through

Phaki, Zana , Nomvuyo and Nosizwe Nokwe

to match us to our chosen-course universities could only have been elaborate. There I was, little Nosizwe who aspired to study chemical engineering in one of the world's oldest oil processing cities! On completion of my diploma, I returned to Zambia in 1984, and there was a different energy and urgency in the air with indications that we would probably be going back home soon, as talks about talks were beginning. During my tenure in Lusaka, I was honoured to work at the office of the Secretary-General at headquarters, right next door to the Office of the President of the ANC. You were very interested in my studies and my plans for the future and always encouraging that I further my studies in preparation for our return to South Africa, emphasising how important my speciality would be for the country, which was such a boost of confidence and a great honour. In 1985, I returned to the USSR, to Moscow, this time to study for my master's; I specialised in the synthesis of petrochemicals. My ultimate dream was to work at Sasol on return to a free South Africa.

The message that was always communicated to us when the different leaders of the ANC came to the Soviet Union was that we were being prepared for when we went back home to South Africa to contribute to the economy and, therefore, had to absorb as much as we could and learn as hard as we could. We knew the emphasis that you placed on education and the role of students

in the liberation struggle. We knew, too, that you laid great emphasis on the importance of integrating students within the broader struggle for freedom

Every year, on 8 January, for the 10 years I was there, we received the 8 January Statement from the ANC Headquarters. We always looked forward to the message from you, Uncle O. R. By then, we had graduated from calling you Uncle to always referring to you as Our President. What an honour to have a president with such vision and inspiration who instilled in us the hope that freedom would be obtained in our lifetime if we all worked together on all the fronts fighting for liberation.

Da zdracvyete cvaboda naroda UR!
Long live the freedom of the people of South Africa!
Da zdractvyete solidarnosti progresivni narodi!
Long live the solidarity of the progressive forces!
Da zdractvyete Mir vcevo mira!
Long live peace the world over!

Nosizwe Nokwe

Dear Uncle O. R.,

What'er the theme, the maiden sang
As if her song could have no ending;
I saw her singing at her work,
And o'er the sickle bending;
I listened, motionless and still;
And, as I mounted up the hill,
The music in my heart I bore,
Long after it was heard no more.

Those lyrical chestnuts from William Wordsworth's 'The Solitary Reaper' were percolating in my mind as I sat down to pen this missive to you, in honour of what is your centenary year. For the music of freedom and justice you sang, we bore, long after it was heard no more. And that is indeed what inspires us to sing a song of protest, as your ministrations, tutelage, and indeed your song of freedom are under siege from a syndicate, the spawn of your own beloved ANC, that has declared war on decency itself. They have forgotten your ministrations and exhortations. Or is it perhaps that the lustre of lucre and material enrichment has vaporised and eviscerated your example? Has your song proven no match against the palpitating terrestrial desires:, the siren song and chime of the cash register, which animates this oligarchy? But we dissent, and in our remonstrance, have unsheathed our pens to telegraph our song of protest.

Writing this note transported me back to the first time I laid eyes on you, as an 18-year-old boy, in December 1981, when you visited us in the Viana encampment, just outside Luanda, after an extended meeting of the National Executive Committee (NEC). You descended upon us with the entire NEC to present to us John Nkadimeng who had just been appointed Secretary of the Revolutionary Council, succeeding Moses Mabhida, who had vacated that role following his appointment as General Secretary of the South African Communist Party. You would also announce to us on that day, the brutal slaying of the great human rights lawyer and patriot, Griffiths Mxenge, by an apartheid death squad. It was on that day that I first espied Thabo Mbeki. He was in a Guayabera (Cuban traditional shirt), cradling his pipe majestically. I remember being struck by his Marvin Gaye-like mien, bearded and a tad reserved. He was sitting next to Jacob Zuma, who was wearing the same shirt. The two of them cut impressive figures. Two strapping dudes. Young, gifted, and Black. What befell that relationship, and ultimately Jacob Zuma, is the stuff of Sisyphean tragedy.

We would meet again in Maseru, almost exactly a year later, after the murderous incursion by the South African Defence Force, which claimed the lives of 42 people, 30 of our own Comrades and 12 Basotho nationals. You came to give those Comrades a fitting send-off as their commander-in-chief, flying into the smouldering belly of the beast, defying all entreaties for you to stay away for your personal safety. That was a profile in courage and love. It helped lift, becalm and restore to health our wounded souls. We would meet again in June the following year in Lusaka. You had been informed that I had been marooned at the airport in Maputo for three days, with little nourishment and ablution, after the Mozambican authorities, bowing to pressure from Pretoria, after the Church Street car bomb, refused transit through their country for ANC cadres. I was flying from Maseru to Lusaka. You sent for me to give me succour and comfort. I remember crystallinely your response, as I related my ordeal: 'I guess many walls will have to break down on our way to freedom.' You said it with such exquisite flair and flourish. That imagery is etched indelibly in my mind.

You once argued that the enemy lacked the capability to destroy the ANC, as the ANC was rooted in the people. You went on to posit that, only the ANC was capable of destroying itself. That seems to be what we are witness to, in Jacob Zuma and his syndicate's brazen 'repurposing' of the movement and our state for personal aggrandisement: the silent coup, as it has been aptly described. Your beloved ANC has turned on itself and its values with bewildering fury. Ritualistic cannibalism has been unleashed.

It is dog-eat-dog inside your beloved movement. Comrade-eat-Comrade. It has been compared to a criminal enterprise.

Now, Uncle O. R., I have never been of the belief that the ANC was an avatar of unimpeachable omniscience, encapsulated in the popular colloquialism, 'The ANC is right, even when wrong.' I have always regarded the transmutation of that canard and conceit into an article of faith that is dangerous for a democracy. For, in a democracy, the people are sovereign, not parties. And, while our people had reposed their trust on the ANC, that had kept the faith, helping lead our people to freedom; by voting for, and keeping the ANC in power for all of 23 years, this year. If the ANC, or at least those who have wormed themselves to its helm, have violated that trust by behaving corruptly and arrogantly, the people must boot it or them out of power. That power was not the ANC's entitlement, it was a reward for faithful service. So, if the ANC has self- destructed, consistent with your admonition (it was not destroyed by the enemy), it clearly is no longer the ANC of the struggle that our people had imbued with the halo of greatness and requisite obeisance. Why should our people reward the programme of betrayal and desecration that those usurpers have embarked upon?

It was no less a personage than your own brother and comrade, Madiba, who exhorted the electorate to kick the ANC out of power if it was no longer faithful to the creed of freedom and justice. I felt the need to communicate the tragic tidings that the organisation that you ably and sagaciously led, has, under the leadership of Jacob Zuma, surrendered the mantle of being a faithful champion of our people's aspirations. Ironically, it could well be that a stint out of power may be exactly what the ANC needs to rediscover its soul and mission.

I suspect that, being the sage that you are, you are not entirely surprised by these tidings. I believe that your response would be that the ANC, born in Mangaung 105 years ago, 5 years before your own birth, fulfilled its historical mission of 'freedom in our lifetime'. Your ANC was never conceived to be a fetish, an object of occultist idolatry warranting prostration and obsequious bedazzlement, but rather an instrument of struggle and liberation. And our task as a free people is to defend the heritage of freedom and justice through our political engagement, rather than futilely romanticising the past. After all, the wise implore us to live in the here and now. Not marinate in the past. I am sure that your response to this Zupta epidemic would be to summon us to the barricades to defend our hard-won democracy, just like you did in that virtuostic peroration in Matola, Mozambique in 1981: 'To battle, Comrades, to battle!'

Amandla!

Oyama Mabandla

SOMAFCO CONTINUED

On O. R. Tambo, uComrade President

My admittedly fragmented recollections of that great man would really be more accurately recorded under the banner 'through the 39-year-old looking glass.'

For me, Comrade President is best remembered through the lens of my parents. I first met him, at the age of eight, at the narrow, pale, salmon-coloured house we called our first home in Maputo. His house in Maputo was around the corner, barely a five-minute walk away. I cannot claim to have an intimate knowledge of that great human being, but I do recall that he travelled only with a driver, no entourage, and opened the rear door of the car to let himself in or out. I refer to him as Comrade President because that's how my Dad referred to him. My mum, on the other hand, simply called him, Bhuti O. R. To my eight-year-old self, he became, and stayed, 'Comrade President'. Somehow that fit with the austere image that I encountered: a serious-looking man in black horn-rimmed spectacles, a full head of hair, and intriguing facial marks I tried hard not to stare at. It was awe-inspiring to shake hands with a 'president' in our own home.

What I also recall, in subsequent encounters with Comrade President, was the greeting smile as he interacted with other ANC adults: it was warm, wide and welcoming. I often watched the ANC Comrades as they interacted, and it was truly remarkable how, irrespective of age or gender, they always greeted each other with deep warmth, love and, most of all, with an evident sense of solidarity that was encompassed in the word that flowed constantly between and among them, 'Comrade'. O. R.'s eyes crinkled up on the outer edges when he smiled, the top part of his cheeks rounded up under his glasses and, for a moment, the distinctive markings on his cheeks were less severe. Those marks had conjured up war in my mind and, I, given to a vivid imagination that feasted on all kinds of books, thought him a warrior of some kind. I later got an explanation from my father that those marks were a unique and familiar cultural practice among the AmaMpondo, the people of whom O. R. Tambo was born.

I don't think there was, in that generation, a leader my dad respected more: it seemed to me that he revered Comrade President. They served together in the National Executive Committee (NEC), of the ANC from 1985–1991. My dad, stationed in Swaziland in the 1960s and 70s, served under the organisation's leadership. It seemed, though, that he was quite often in close contact with the Comrade President. I pointedly remember the day my dad told me that it was time that he, my dad, left Swaziland.

I pleaded with him to stay. He said that his departure had been commanded by uComrade President. Well, that was the end of my tear-filled pleas. I understood that, when uComrade President set a particular direction, there was nothing more to be said.

To my Mum, 'Bhuti O. R.' was an older brother and Comrade whom she regarded with respect and affection. She fondly recalls that her *mngqusho* (a tasty indigenous South African dish of samp and sugar beans, spiced in her unique way) was quite a winner with him. That must have been a lovely reminder of home, to have *mngqusho* when so far away. I think it would be fair to say that they shared a mutual respect and admiration, for they would speak at length whenever he came by our home, usually about politics and the state of the southern African region. There were also lighter moments, and I still remember how my mum exclaimed with pleasure at the gift Bhuti O. R. gave her upon his return to Maputo from a trip somewhere. It was a bottle of 'Worth', a perfume in a dainty little bottle. I regularly explored my mum's cosmetics, and I discovered that, even though the Worth bottle looked nicer, I much preferred the scent of Mary Quant in its practical cylindrical canister. Interestingly, that childhood influence lingers: today, I much prefer floral scents to subtle musky notes.

It was normal for Regional Political Committee (RPC) meetings to take place in our home. Not surprisingly, when Comrade President was in town, ALL the members of the RPC made it to the meeting! Whenever he was in town, the ANC and the South African community seemed to experience a surge of renewal, the political fervour increased, and the resolve to fight harder for our freedom seemed to strengthen. His very presence inspired and, even as little Pioneers, we performed with greater zeal, reciting the Freedom Charter flawlessly!

So, what would I say to that dedicated, disciplined paragon on the occasion of his 100th birthday? Here goes:

I so wish for your grandchildren that they could spend whole days with you and just listen to you speak of your life, your family, the lessons you have learned, and what you wish for them.

If I could spend a whole day with you (and Ms Maya Angelou), well, I would ask: what did you love best, and what did you find hurt the most, during your time on earth?

I would share with you that you (the leadership collective) and the ANC frequently broke my heart, and that I always forgave that heartbreak because I understood that the liberation struggle was bigger than all of us.

I would also share with you that getting to meet you and President Samora Machel have got to be among the best, most inspirational moments of my life as an eight-year-old. I will never forget either one of those moments: mine, all mine. As I look back at that eight-year-old girl with shiny brown skin, happy eyes,

and thick, nearly unmanageable braids, my breath catches in my throat. I was not gleeful; I was awed and I was inspired. I was also determined to grow up and do something that would be worthy of the liberation struggle ethos and values evident in O. R. Tambo and Samora Machel. You see, you were, in that order, my greatest heroes: my dad, then you, Comrade President, and then Samora Machel. I was about to complete my final year of high school when I heard on the news that President Samora Machel had been killed. I cried alone in that sterile boarding school, mourning the death of greatness in a way that I was unable to articulate. It seemed to me, then, that not only President Machel had died, but, in a way, Mozambique had too. I remember wishing I was in Mozambique to be among, and mourn with, Mozambicans at that time.

Similarly, in mid-April 1993, I was far away from home when you, Comrade President, died. The quiet assurances my dad gave me then about where the negotiations were going in South Africa were similar to the conversation he had with me when he called to say that one of my favourite uncles, Chris Hani, had been killed. Then, I had immediately set out to return home only to be halted by my dad with reassurance after reassurance that civil war had not broken out. When you passed on, Comrade President, all I longed for was to be home in the solidarity of Comrades.

I would lastly share with you, Comrade President, that the golden thread among my heroes remains unbroken. Ironically, 10 years after you passed, I was again far from home when my Dad passed on. I said my farewells to four of the greatest human beings I have been privileged to meet, to know, and to hold dear, from afar: alone, away from the solidarity of Comrades. The values and teaching you embodied help us today to navigate this earth and to strive to mould, in our own children, citizens of the world whom you, too, would applaud. As we applauded you all.

I retain the awe. And the inspiration. And, I treasure the memories. Mine. All mine.

With deepest respect,

Phola Palesa Mabizela-Mabaso

Dearest Uncle O. R.,

Though I am told by my parents that you were part of my life from birth, my first conscious and vivid recollection of time spent with you was at the age of 9 years. We were at one of our regular ANC cultural evenings in Mazimbu (Tanzania). The hall was packed and you were seated in the front row. Very hard to miss! On delivering the last line 'for you have an exorbitant price to pay!' – (a reference to Verwoerd) of my poetry recital, you rose and gave me an extended standing ovation. Your excited applause and beaming smile, which broke into laughter when our eyes met, filled me with a never-to-be-forgotten sense of pride and achievement! For the rest of that trip, I walked around with a puffed-up sense of self-importance because you had told me that I was a 'star performer' who would one day use my skills in a meaningful way for the benefit of our people. For the remainder of your time in Mazimbu, I became your little shadow, following wherever you went. The warm grasp of your firm hand, your kind and ready smile, and your patience in explaining, over and over again, why we were gathered in exile, are key components of my lasting memories of my holidays in Mazimbu. However, as a child born in exile, what I relished most were the tales you told of growing up in the village of Kantolo in the Eastern Cape, how you made your way to Johannesburg, and your years of practising law at Chancellor House with Nelson Mandela, and my father, Mendi Msimang, as your clerk. For me, you painted a very real picture of what this country called South Africa looked, smelt and felt like.

You had a special way with us children, and we in turn were captivated by your passion, eloquence and warmheartedness. In retrospect, I am struck by how down to earth you were, given the enormity of your global role and responsibilities within, and for, the ANC. You had time for us all, enquiring, encouraging and reminding us of our rich history and heritage, as well as our obligation to one day guard and defend our freedom, and to continuously struggle in order to see progress. Following from your lessons to us as children, today I understand this progress to mean striving for social justice in order to ensure the dignity of all.

As I grew up you remained a regular feature of my life, always warmhearted and finding the time to listen and encourage, whether in Dar es Salaam, Lusaka or in London where, sadly, I became a witness to your failing health. Even then you were still accessible to everyone. Reflecting on the time you devoted to being with, and teaching, children and young people in Mazimbu and elsewhere, I now see it as your putting into practice your firmly held belief that our movement did not deserve a future if it did not value its youth and children.

I will never forget the day you decided to do an on-the-spur-of-

the-moment, in loco, inspection of my family at 'Corner B', the humble, single room we occupied in a four-bedroomed dust-, mould-, mosquito- and cockroach-infested house in Keko, Dar es Salaam. You had been under the impression that our family lived in the lap of luxury, as a consequence of many reports sent to you to this effect. The reality of our miserable living conditions reduced you to tears. Your ability to feel others' pain was a lesson I hold dear to this day. Our pain at the sense of injustice was your pain.

You were heavily on my mind on the day of our country's first democratic elections in 1994, as I stood in the voting queue. I felt sad at your absence, especially recalling the significant role you had played in ensuring that one day, in my lifetime, I would be exercising my democratic right to vote. As I cast my vote, I promised you that I would continue to uphold the values by which you lived, and to always speak my mind, as loudly and clearly, as you had always encouraged us to do.

At this time, I share with many a deep sense of shame, anger, confusion and disappointment with how the democratic project has unfolded in part, shifting from one catastrophe to the next 'Inyakanyaka' as my mother would have described it, while shaking her head in dismay. But during the moments of despair, I

always recall the example of your life, and my privilege at having been exposed to you as much as I was. My many memories of you compel me to strive, every day, to turn this deep seated anger into a powerful force for good and social justice. The struggle is indeed a never-ending process, and for me, your teachings echo in the reminder from the late Coretta Scott King, who would have turned ninety this week, that: 'freedom is never really won, you earn it and win it in every generation'.

Thank you so much Uncle OR, for dedicating your life to the struggle for our liberation with such grace and wisdom. May you rest in peace knowing that our generation of South Africans will keep the embers of the struggle glowing, as we continue to strive to create a truly united democratic and non-racial society.

Happy 100th Birthday!

With comradely love and affection,

Pulane Kingston

Dearest President O. R. Tambo,

Having spent copious amounts of time pondering what I could pen today that might interest Kaizana, our skilled and gallant leader from Bizana/Kantolo in Pondoland and, following considerable reflection, I reasoned that it would be correct to begin by echoing our nation's recognition of what you and your virtuous family, among other heroes and heroines, braved in sustaining our people's struggle against the immoral scheme of apartheid. I knew that I could also take the opportunity to echo South Africa's loud voice of collective and immeasurable gratitude for the weight you carried in pledging your life to, and, for decades, leading the institution that is the African National Congress toward the just cause of liberation for all.

Further, and inspired, Comrade President, by your standing belief in the then young among the body of cadres and by a quote carried in Luli Callinicos's book, *Beyond the Engeli Mountains*, where your good and dear friend, Archbishop Trevor Huddleston, persuasively articulates that, 'History is never simply a chronicle of the past. It is always a challenge to contemporary thought for the future.' I thought it valuable to share with you a perspective on the state of our nation today, its relationship with the past, and consequence for the future.

Inferring, President, that the moment of liberation in countries that experienced colonialism and oppression, like ours, was never in itself an end but rather a means in the pursuit for equality and prosperity for ALL citizens, and that the founding fathers of the African National Congress, John Dube and his co-visionaries prior to and post 1912, your generation and all partakers in-between, strived, in pursuit of that so principled a concept. In an uncompromised rejection of the horrid monster that is colonialism and against the moment's generally perceived prospect of failure, courageous men and women across our continent, and beyond, brought to being and nourished institutions of resistance: liberation movements that traversed generations and that, with the passage of time, succeeded in the cause and liberated their various peoples.

With freedom achieved and consequential triumph at the polls, the African National Congress took control of the pedals of national power. Having attained that seminal milestone, the ANC, like many institutions of liberation before it, was inopportunely unsuccessful in recognising the need to recalibrate, to birth and nurture new institutional capacity that would correspondingly march toward delivering the so-craved prosperity to the majority of South Africans. We remained convinced that, through the liberation movement, our aspiration to deliver equity to society would be achieved through existing state capacity. In other words, we could, through apartheid's institutional architecture, disentangle our people's challenges. As a consequence, per my interpretation at least, in hundreds of years and not having created new capacity, the ANC remains, in truth, the solitary institution of import that truly belongs to our people.

This president is relevant because I am certain that you would be troubled that, as a direct consequence, we have moved painfully slowly to transform patterns of livelihood in our country, and that the gap between wealthy and poor is expanding persistently, and most perturbingly, along racial lines.

Within that setting, and because of its control over the vast resources of the State, your celebrated organisation's president has evolved to become the center of patronage. I am sad to report, Sir, that the ANC, as the primary plank on which power destinies are carved, is resultantly a platform that now experiences renewing brawls for its very soul.

To you, the elders who saw, we ask.

Ronnie Ntuli

Dear Comrade O. R.,

A few years ago, I had a breakfast with a South African intelligence officer who told me that he knew you well. Over runny eggs, he spoke of having been groomed in far-off countries by your steady hand. He recalled fondly some of your sayings and mannerisms, eventually regaling me with a story of how, one day, during the long exile years, you had gathered a few comrades at closed quarters to address a matter that had been on your mind for some time.

My companion looked wistfully into the distance as he paused to give effect to his story. Apparently, you'd paused in that way before looking around the room and finally asking, in hushed tones, 'What is to be done when we have won our liberation ... and ... eventually, the ANC becomes corrupted by power?'

I nearly snorted out my orange juice. 'What? Really? He asked that?' I looked at the raconteur quizzically.

He nodded and then went on to describe how emphatic you were about an answer being found to that very critical question.

There was obviously shock and a lot of mirth in the room. At the time, the apartheid state was at its most repressive. It was difficult to imagine it being dislodged, regardless of how courageously optimistic the struggle slogans of the time were.

Just imagining the ANC in power was, then, mental gymnastics – any realist could have correctly reflected on the countless decades 'freedom' had been promised and, like an absentee father, ultimately not arrived. What a preposterous thought that the ANC of Luthuli could become corrupted like the governments of those African despots that suckled on the imperialist American teat. The idea that the ANC, which had always been on the right side of history, and the people could go the other way was clearly laughable to many in the room. And yet, it seemed as inevitable to you as the rising of the sun in the East.

I found myself nodding understandingly. 'That clearly meant that President O. R. had been paying attention to the trajectory of liberation and progressive nationalist movements across Africa and the world, and noted how quickly many slid into the bad habits of the repressive regimes they replaced, right?' I searched my compatriot's face for confirmation of my super-spot-on guess, but he simply sucked his teeth, shook his head slightly, and exhaled the 'I don't know ... he just knew'.

With that, he switched tack, brought up another story from the past, laughed a little and then excused himself. He had something urgent to get to. Perhaps a regime change witch-hunt. I sat around a little, mulling over some of the things he'd told me.

Having been raised in the grand tradition of paranoia that revolutionary movements bequeath their children, I was obviously a little skeptical. First, I wondered about my companion's views and motives for telling me that story – he was an intelligence officer after all! Don't they orchestrate 'concerns' to locate their subject's perspectives? I pondered that, not that there was much to locate: Google could have pointed him to articles with my views on the decay of the ANC.

Moreover, I was skeptical about whether that chap was even in the room when that incident occurred or if that story was yet another mythical folk tale about the amazing O. R. I'd encountered many such tales all of my life, the earliest fed to me by own my grandmother, MaMsimang – you used to fondly call her Aggie, remember? – who would tell stories of your valour, wisdom and spellbinding voice by candlelight.

All of that aside, I strangely didn't question the notion that you would have raised that particular question. That you, Comrade O. R., would have predicted that, one day, the glorious movement of the people would become a villainous lecherous parasite feasting on the hope and goodwill of the people was in keeping with your character. You were a thoughtful, wise man with foresight. And so, I decided that, if the incident that the intelligence officer had told me about had taken place, you'd known what the future held in

store for our beloved movement because old people tend to know things.

In time, I began to rethink that. Over the past decade, more and more has emerged about the dark underbelly of the movement in exile: hidden tales, once told only in hushed tones, are now written about in books or spoken about at dinner in the same breath as 'pass the salt, tu'. They paint a disheartening picture of an ANC afflicted by corruption, even then: an ANC where the abuse of power and sexual assault were uneasy bedfellows with torture and selling out. Every such account adds a whiff of rancidity to the wonderfully warm and reassuring porridge of propaganda that children born into the ANC, as I was, were raised on. Perhaps, I began to think, you knew that the ANC today would be corrupt because you knew then just how morally bankrupt leading figures in the ANC really were.

Is that the case?

If so, then it becomes clearer that the ANC I grew up in was merely a work of fiction. A painting drawn, coloured in, and held up by you as its painter-in-chief. That painting was awash with unity and singularity of purpose, of selflessness and service. It had bold strokes of equity, democracy and justice, and covered over the paper cracks of ignobility and lies. But the colors are faded.

There has been no attempt to varnish it and preserve the artwork. It is lying in some office of some official somewhere, sandwiched between an old cardboard 1994 election poster and a framed picture of you alongside Comrades Mandela and Sisulu. Forgotten. No one even remembers that that painting lies gathering dust where it does.

There has always been something rotten, hasn't there, Comrade O. R.?

And yet, through it all, never have I heard anyone speak ill of you. Or insinuate in anyway that you were involved in nefarious goings on: theft, sexual abuse in the camps, torture. I often wonder how it is, though, that your name is never implicated in the unseemly things reported to have happened in exile, and yet you did not eradicate them. Was it to preserve 'unity'? Was it the price of not wanting to split and fracture the movement?

If so, I'd like to let you know how closely that example is being followed. Yes, out of everything to emulate, not holding our people to account tops the list. Today, accountability exists in the ANC only for political expediency. But if indeed accountability was sacrificed on the altar of unity in a time of extreme danger, that surely doesn't apply now, when the ANC is at the forefront of political power. Unity, however, is often a rallying call to cover up

misdeeds and move on.

Did you know that this would be an eventual outcome? And if not, could it have been foreseen and averted? How, Comrade O. R.? How?

And how do we proceed? Knowing that things must be corrected but that the public proxy wars over principles are damaging the movement. Is it worth the fight and the noise? Or is the ANC worth protecting while protecting crooks posing to be comrades; like askaris posing to be soldiers while literally feeding poison to their compatriots?

Mac Maharaj once quoted your friend and comrade, my grandfather, Walter Sisulu, in explaining that there were two struggles in the days before freedom: one was the struggle for liberation, and the other was the struggle to mould the vehicle driving the struggle for liberation. I found that idea instructive: it gave me the comfort that battles within the movement based on principle are necessary for the continued ability of the movement to lead the struggle for the betterment of people's lives. I do wonder, often, just how bitter and acrimonious those battles can be before there is no longer a movement. And what if the so-called progressive forces lose?

In conversations with many elders, some of whom worked alongside you for many years, I detect the notion that one cannot rescue the ANC by participating in the things that are destroying it, such as vote buying, membership, structural manipulation and dirty tricks campaigns. But those methodologies are now the de facto mechanisms for delivering leadership and policy. They are the dominant culture. How do you change that without adapting to the tactics of the day? Is fighting dirty to win and clean things up not a worthwhile form of struggle over the vehicle of struggle? Does the end not justify the means? Or do the means determine how things end?

Am I being too Hamlet-y?

Recently, a few weeks after I started writing this letter to you, I stumbled across another old tale with you at the centre. On an underground mission, you rebuked your cohorts, the story goes, as they arrived to pick you up in a stolen car. One of the men had stolen it because the car you were all meant to use had broken down somewhere. That, the narrator told me, wasn't reason enough for you to get in. Apparently, you started to walk, all the while reminding your companions of their obligations to remain morally upright in struggle.

I guess that answers some of my earlier questions. It reminds me of a memory my father once shared with me about travelling from one country to another with a suitcase full of dollars. It was money for operations, and when he wasn't picked up at the appointed place at the appointed time, he walked, for kilometers on end, even though he had enough money to pay for a taxi. No one would have known.

I remember thinking at the time that the world then was very different; people did the right thing more easily back then. But now, thinking more deeply on those two tales, I realise that the reason I even remember them or that they were told is precisely because doing the right thing wasn't easier. It would have been easier for one to just get into the car. And that's it. There wouldn't be a story. That moment wouldn't have been memorable and perhaps something else that happened that day would be recalled many years later. But certainly, not you getting into the car. That's normal. Presumably, you got into many cars. I've never heard of all the other times. That time was different because you did something different. You did what an ordinary man wouldn't.

I know now that the things that define us are the everyday decisions where going with the grain, getting into a stolen car in a time of resistance, chaos and armed struggled, wouldn't be frowned upon.

I think I understand a little more why you were so admired.

Over the years, people around you were so proud to be around you, to have been in your midst. About a decade ago, an aunty left the ANC to join Cope. She was one of its founding luminaries. She called me over to convince me to join her. She spoke of the values of the movement. She spoke of growing up under your tutelage and recalled what you represented. I respectfully declined to join her new adventure with a sombre 'I will think about it'. Just before I left, she thrust a large white envelope into my hand. In it was what I have since discovered to be an heirloom for many children like me who grew up in the ANC: a picture of you surrounded by dozens of kids, Masupatsela, and I remember the day that we took it: in Lusaka, one warm Saturday afternoon. We had just performed. You were beaming that day with joy and pride, I think. I remember you were very hopeful about what we'd be in a new South Africa. I remember the excitement among the adults who ran our Masupatsela programme and that of many of the older kids who, 'til this day, shine brightly up from the photograph. I always chuckle to myself when I see my young self in the picture. I'm in the picture but am not looking at the camera: I'm in the back pointing at something in the sky. I'm distracted in the presence of so much greatness and joy and hope and am missing the moment ... like our beloved ANC today ...

I often wonder: how did you focus on the main thing with so many reasons to be distracted? Such as the cult-like exaltation of you.

I was told a story the other day of how you stopped the singing in a big meeting when the attendees broke into song about you. You said that that sort of thing leads to cults of personalities. You asked Comrades to sing something else. I nodded furiously when I was told that. It's the right sort of lesson. It was only much later that I realised the irony in that the person who told me that story was, a decade ago, leading Comrades in songs in the name of Comrade Zuma just before the Polokwane Conference.

I suppose that answers my earlier question about winning without principles.

That leads me to another question about leadership: how should we be picking them now? And how should we be preparing for what sort of leaders to be? Why do we only yield leadership to an old man? The symbolism? Why not a younger man or woman? Why did your generation have to lead us into the first free and fair elections? Was it the readiness of your generation? Why wouldn't future generations want that privilege for themselves: a nearly 40-year span at the helm? It's almost biblical – 40 years in the desert ... but even Moses couldn't enter the promised land. Today,

40 years is the age difference between our leader and the leaders of the opposition, give or take a few years.

I think the leadership conveyor belt is a failed mechanism. It's one reason that our revolutionaries eat their infants.

Those are some of the questions swirling in my mind most times. They rushed to the forefront when I sat down to write this. They didn't come alone, they brought many friends, and many, many more questions like:

How did you hold it all together? What happens when the ANC no longer serves its purpose? Does it implode and disappear like the NP to have its DNA resurface in the actions of other organisations? We already see how every political party organises like yours did. Will it fade into irrelevance like the PAC, splitting itself ad infinitum into nothingness? Will it be able to find its way back? Or will it become authoritarian like Zanu? What happens to the void in the middle – that space between the dying and the dead and the next thing to replace it?

'Always prepared to defend my people, my country and my organisation.' You taught us that mantra. Do you remember? And, like everything we were indoctrinated with, it seems a time capsule for the future. A future in which you were certain we would emerge victorious before descending into chaos. The priority is clear here: the people before the organisation.

Another answer from your deeds. It's uncanny. Did you know I was going to ask those questions?

Maybe, just maybe, if we study your ways and writings, we will find the answer to the question you posed: 'What is to be done when we have won our liberation ... and ... the ANC becomes corrupted by power?'

My love to Comrade Adelaide, please tell her that her second husband misses her.

Comradely yours,

Shaka Sisulu

O. R. Tambo International Airport

Uncle O. R. had tickly whiskers. I remember his face up close, the scratch of those long stubbornly curly hairs on my impish little face. I remember his laugh and how his eyes would crinkle on the sides and those crinkles would match the topsy-turvy moustache that looked like twigs to my imaginative mind.

Uncle O. R. was a beautiful tree that sometimes sat on our couch. When the tree was tired, it would stand up and go and lie down and sleep in the room Mummy had set up for him. I remember how everybody looked at that tree: as though they were grateful for its cooling shade and for the branches that extended far above their heads. He did not seem to know he was a tree, even though everyone else sitting under the shelter of his presence did.

Uncle O. R. was never the one who spoke the most or the loudest. Others did that, and he listened and nodded and smiled. Uncle O. R. smiled a lot. You could tell by the way everyone looked at him, though – even the loud ones who liked the sound of their own voices – how much they loved being near the quiet tree sitting on the settee.

When you are a very small child – if you are lucky – you take love for granted, for you are the centre of the universe. When you are the very small child of people who are soldiers, you learn big words very quickly. You learn words with big meanings like *uMkhonto we Sizwe*, liberation, a luta continua, and would say those words with great care and proper enunciation. Watching the smiles of the adults, you would see the twigs on Uncle O. R.'s face move up and down in laughter when you raised your fist in the air, squeaking *Amandla*! and he claps. The words have big meanings but you are only little and, when Uncle O. R. smiles and puts you on his lap, all you know is the words become love.

Sometimes, you have some hint of an idea that your little world has been deliberately created to shelter you from something far away that would harm you if it could. Your world is luminous but the big words with big meanings also tell you something the adults won't say, which is that your world is also fragile. You don't know how to put a finger on that: it is a current that tugs at your heart: an ebb and flow that tells you that the universe is bigger than you can presently imagine.

When you are old enough, you learn how to put yourself into context. Isn't that the bittersweetness of growing up? That we learn how to gauge our place in the world in relation to others and events? It is both necessary and heartbreaking to accept that one is not the centre of the universe. The end of innocence paves the road for the beginning of wisdom.

Even so, that luminous and fragile community – Lusaka – never disappears from memory. The idea of being important – of being somebody – that sense that Uncle O. R. created and the adults around us sustained – never fades. The coolness of the shade under that tree with tickly twigs and the peal of Uncle O. R.'s laughter; the sweetness of being acknowledged: those are the memories that carry you through when others doubt you.

The future has arrived and now you are a grown woman living in a democratic South Africa. You travel overseas a lot because you have a good job. You are one of the lucky ones: one of those for whom freedom has delivered.

As the plane begins to descend, the pilot makes an announcement. 'Ladies and gentlemen, as we prepare for landing, we just want to make a note. When we left the other day, we departed from Jan Smuts Airport. Today, as we land, we're flying into the newly named Oliver Reginald Tambo Airport.'

The plane is full of people who did not know Oliver Tambo, so there was no applause. The travellers are still sleepy; many of them are not South Africans. They do not understand what the renaming means and, so, for a moment, you are struck by an almost unbearable loneliness. You are the only one on that plane to have sat on his lap and played with his whiskers.

You look down, down, down into the darkness. You look at the city twinkling beneath you. You look at the place your heart always longed for, the South Africa you are still making a home. You look at it all, and you cry because the centre of the universe has shifted, but the memories have not faded, and the taste of your tears has never changed, just as the sound of his laughter is a statue erected in your mind's eye, and for a moment. you don't dare to blink.

Uncle O. R.'s greatest lesson to us all was that we were important even when the powerful would have preferred us to doubt our own importance. That is a lesson – luminous and fragile and more resilient than we might have guessed – that shines across the ages.

Sisonke Msimang

Dear Uncle O. R.,

In the early years, you used to come and give us talks at the Masupatsela Club, our Saturday school, which was like a political school for ANC children. Over time, you had more demands on your time and couldn't visit The Club as frequently. The lessons and values you instilled in us were cornerstones of the ANC's principles: courage, humility, self-respect, integrity, loyalty and goodwill to all men (comradeship). Importantly, you taught us about hard work, especially in our studies, and self-discipline. 'Discipline' was a word very often used in the ANC during the exile years.

One time in the early 1980s, we had the honour of performing South African traditional song and dance at the beautiful Lusaka State House (residence of the Zambian President), where you were honoring Zambia's Freedom Day celebrations with Dr Kenneth Kaunda. You had given one of your resounding speeches (your oratory skills are well documented) when we took to the stage and the Zambian National Broadcasting Corporation cameras were rolling … being a child, that was all so exciting! And as little as we were, we felt part of the important publicity work and solidarity movement of the struggle!

I ended up studying law. Truth be told, finishing my A levels at the age of 18, I didn't really know what I wanted to do as a career but knew I wanted to make a difference in our country when it was free one day. My parents advised me that a legal degree would be a 'safe bet' and was quite versatile with the disciples of research, building an argument, looking at things from both sides objectively, and would teach me written and oral skills. I could always decide later what to study for a masters or a specialisation. Having made that choice, I was lucky to excel, especially in the areas of human rights and jurisprudence.

Having been home after graduation, just before our first democratic elections in 1994, I realised that, with the best constitution in the world and a leading bill of human rights, after democracy, those rights would have no meaning if our people couldn't exercise them. If they couldn't afford decent homes or give their children a good education, what real difference would simply now having a vote mean, practically, in improving their lives? That's when I decided to study business and economics at the master's level and go into the world of investment banking and finance where I felt decisions about funding development and opening up and growing South Africa's economy could really make a difference to our people's lives.

The blessing of earning scholarships for my studies in top universities would not have been possible without the

international goodwill built by our leadership under Tata O. R. for children like us, whose families had no means. That, combined with hard work and a vision for making a difference in a free South Africa, added resilience and tenacity, even in trying times, as a poor student in foreign lands.

My heart bursts with appreciation for all the rich memories, despite the difficulty of the circumstances and the very unconventional upbringing we had. You held the bigger ANC family together. We Masupatselas hope and pray that you can hear and receive our thanks and wishes of never-ending blessings to you Tata, O. R. We will never stop loving you, our country or the Real ANC. We need your spirit now more than ever before. *Lala noxolo*, our beloved Tata O. R.

Sonja de Bruyn Sebotsa

Top: Sonja's father, Henry Benny Nato De Bruyn with O. R.
Above: Sonja with her mum Sophia, her sister Danielle and her niece Kayla

Dear O. R. Tambo,

This year marks the centenary of your birth, and honouring that affords us an opportunity to celebrate your life and achievements, which were many and profound. Of all the leaders of the liberation struggle, your unique contribution is arguably one of the least recognised or widely understood. I'm sure that's not something that would concern you: you were far too modest; you always put the struggle before any personal ambition or need for recognition. However, there are other reasons for believing that your deeds should be more widely celebrated. Not to make a hero of you, although that would not be unwarranted, but because your life, your values and your leadership qualities were exemplary and set a standard by which current and future leaders might be measured.

Your soft-spoken and patient manner, combined with a steely determination and masterful political analysis, left little purchase for the predictable demonisation and vilification of the establishment media. A man with such humility, compassion and intelligence could not successfully be portrayed as a monster.

From humble beginnings, you took the challenge of building international solidarity to undreamt of heights: you were the architect of arguably the largest and most successful single-issue movement of the twentieth century. You garnered support from millions of private citizens across Europe and North America, sympathetic Scandinavian governments, the socialist countries – particularly the former USSR and Cuba, other African nations, including, and often at great cost to themselves, the Frontline States and, ultimately, the United Nations.

That inclusivity was reflected within the ANC itself, which provided a welcoming home for progressive people of all races and even multiple nationalities. Not only was that the right thing to do morally, politically and strategically, it belied the hostile narrative of the struggle as some kind of race war that sought only to supplant one kind of racial supremacy with another. Similarly, you ensured that the ANC was non-sexist, affording women an equal opportunity to contribute their full talents to the struggle.

Without all of that, the struggle against apartheid would never have assumed the global prominence that it did, becoming a defining human rights issue that created a clear distinction between those who yearned for a better world based on equality and those who looked to history to normalise colonialism, racism and ethnic supremacy. In Britain, it brought our imperial past into sharper focus and helped to drive casual racism fully into the realm of the socially unacceptable.

Within South Africa, you managed to keep the struggle alive against enormous odds and to assimilate and unite the various spontaneous uprisings against the injustices of apartheid under a common banner and a common cause, eventually to form a broad and overwhelming consensus for change that transcended generations, class and race. The challenge to the State, in the end, was total: culturally isolated, economically boycotted, militarily defeated, morally repugnant and unable any longer to enforce compliance through fear, violence and intimidation.

Even though I was born 50 years later than you and thousands of miles away from South African shores, you had a profound effect on my life too. Without you, I would never have been offered the opportunity to contribute to the transformation of South Africa, an act which, at the time, was done selflessly and on principle but which has since given my life meaning and rewarded me in ways I could never have imagined. Although we never met in person, your hand guided every aspect of that project and brought it to a successful conclusion.

It was a tragedy that you never lived to see your life's work come to fruition, to see apartheid finally fall with your own eyes as South Africans cast their ballots in 1994, but being reunited with your long lost comrades and friends freed from Robben Island in the years previously must have been a clear indication that change was indeed inevitable, and that the continuation of the struggle rested in safe hands. As they were the first to acknowledge, without your efforts, their sacrifices could have been in vain and their names lost to history for who knows how many more years to come.

Your legacy is unquantifiable, it's growth exponential, added to by each child who is born free to explore their full potential, unfettered by restrictions imposed upon them by racial classification and colonial exploitation. While it's certainly true that, even today, much remains to be done to fully realise your dream of economic freedom for the people of South Africa, your efforts ensured that the tools to make that transformation rest in the hands of the people to do with as they see fit in decades to come, and your life, your values, and principles provide a wealth of wisdom and inspiration to guide them.

You didn't only succeed in changing South Africa, you helped to change the world.

Stuart Round
London, 2017

Oliver Tambo – The epitome of exemplary leadership

Exile is strangely compelling to think about but terrible to experience. It is the unhealable rift forced between a human being and a native place, between the self and its true home: its essential sadness can never be surmounted. And while it is true that literature and history contain heroic, romantic, glorious, even triumphant episodes in an exile's life, these are no more than efforts meant to overcome the crippling sorrow of estrangement. The achievements of exile are permanently undermined by the loss of something left behind forever. — Edward W. Said, *Reflections on Exile: And Other Literary and Cultural Essays,* Kindle Location 3493, Granta Publications, Kindle Edition.

Often when we remember and eulogise Oliver Reginald Tambo as an exceptional leader, it is often overlooked and possibly not even considered that his feat of triumph over adversity was achieved under conditions of exile where 'the glorious, even triumphant episodes in an exile's life, [amount to] no more than efforts meant to overcome the crippling sorrow of estrangement ... the loss of something left behind forever'.

O. R. Tambo left South Africa in 1960 following a decision of the ANC in 1959 that he and Comrade Josia Matlou must leave the country. Their instructions were to 'to rally international support for the isolation of the apartheid state' and to 'create a reliable rear base' for the struggle. Oliver Tambo left the country only a week after the traumatic Sharpville massacre and just before the ANC and the PAC were banned. The Sharpville Massacre marked a turning point in the struggle against apartheid and changed the course of history for the country and the people involved in the execution of the struggle against apartheid.

It was at that point that the intransigence and arrogance of the apartheid authorities became firmly entrenched, secure in the conviction that they would rule South Africa and the indigenous people for over a thousand years.

That obstinate attitude of the apartheid regime was a product of their self-delusion and false belief in their might and invincibility, and that theirs was a God-ordained right to rule over the people of our country.

But it was also a serious miscalculation by the white supremacists and a manifestation of their utter contempt for the capacity, the resilience and resolve on the part of the oppressed to throw off the yoke of oppression from their shoulders.

The countervailing force to white arrogance became personified in the bravery and heroism of those who chose the turbulence, deprivation and uncertainties of exile life to break the shackles and the chains of bondage from their ankles.

That resolve expressed in the manifesto of *Umkhonto we Sizwe*, which declared 'The time comes in the life of any nation when there remain only two choices: submit or fight' was born of a deep conviction that injustice and oppression can never prevail over justice and freedom. The enjoyment of freedom and justice is, by definition, the natural order of the state of being human.

The resolve to escalate the struggle to the level of armed resistance and the spirit of no surrender found expression and was personified in the preparedness of those brave men and women 'to overcome the crippling sorrow of estrangement' and endure the ever-present pain of exile and the numbing and almost paralysing yearning for home and 'the loss of something left behind forever'.

Oliver Tambo became the pioneer and trailblazer who was given the task to climb and reach the summit of the psychological Mount Kilimanjaro of the debilitating effects of exile and inspire all of those following after him that it could be done.

O. R. recalls that they (with Yusuf Dadoo) were the first freedom fighters from South Africa to be received by that 'great son of Africa', Mwalimu Nyerere, in then Tanganyika. He made the point that those early days were 'hopeful and exciting' but were also 'particularly frugal ones when we often did not know where the next meal was coming from'.

Oliver Tambo belongs to that galaxy of leaders produced in the heat of the struggle against oppression and human degradation. The question that we must answer, not for academic reasons but because we must learn from it and strive to emulate O. R. Tambo's leadership in the service of our people, is: 'What makes O. R. Tambo stand out as a beacon and shining star of exemplary leadership within that galaxy of leaders?'

Those of us in exile who had the privilege to experience the leadership of Oliver Tambo and those who had the opportunity to interact with him in his capacity as the president of the ANC are in agreement that Tambo was in a class of his own.

As the director of Radio Freedom, I also had the privilege of experiencing O. R. Tambo's leadership first hand and at close proximity. That sustained me, and I look back to the days of exile with a sense of pride and a feeling that, even as I experienced the trauma and vicissitudes of exile life, it was a time well spent, it was a time spent in self-discovery and the definition of the self and my purpose in life.

In order to give context to O.R Tambo's leadership, as I understand it, I will locate him within four categories of leadership. The first of those is Tambo the inspirational leader; second, Tambo as the visionary leader; third, Tambo as a servant of the people, and last but not least, Tambo as a down-to-earth and unassuming father figure.

Those qualities of leadership, as I have observed them, tend to overlap: they are not mutually exclusive but rather they should be seen as complimentary and mutually reinforcing. In order to give substance to my observations, I will use anecdotes in an attempt to remove them from the realm of theory and locate them squarely within the realm of practice.

O. R. continues to live in our hearts and minds because he achieved what few people manage to achieve. For him to be an inspirational leader, he was convinced of his personal mission and the purpose of his life.

He believed in a cause, and that belief was firmly entrenched by certain guiding principles and values.
Those values can be summed up as (but not limited to): a deeply rooted love for his people; a strong conviction and belief in the right of freedom and justice; that he must at all times live his life with honesty and trustworthiness and be guided by a set of moral and ethical values. As a source of inspiration, O. R. made all of us believe that victory against oppression was achievable, and that

what you may perceive as impossible is within easy reach. He was the one who would not let you climb Mount Everest alone but would always be there beside you, to encourage you and, if need be, to carry you to the summit of your heart's desire and make you believe that you did that through your own effort.

The place was Makeni, the Headquarters of the Department of Information in Lusaka, and the occasion was a meeting in which President Tambo and other members of the National Executive Committee of the ANC had come to brief the membership about the prospects of a negotiated settlement and the negotiating position of the ANC as reflected in the Harare Declaration. By that time, O. R. had been hit by a stroke and was frail.

But he conducted the meeting and was the one who briefed us. In the end, what he said was memorable and a source of great inspiration to all who were there. He said, 'Comrades, I am no longer as strong and healthy as I used to be, but I would like to assure you that whatever little energy remains in me will be consumed together with you in struggle.' At that moment, there was a deathly silence among the Comrades present as everyone thought deeply about those words. Each one present felt that O. R. had struck a nerve and were inspired by his words. Deep inside ourselves, we knew that fear and doubt, despondency and retreat were not options: failure was not an option, and that the fate of the people of South Africa, our leaders in prison and us was inextricably bound with the survival of Oliver Tambo. That, for me, represented true leadership.

Oliver Tambo believed so strongly in the final victory of the struggle against apartheid. Yet, at the same time, he was under no illusion about the enormity of the struggle and the price of that struggle.

On one occasion, I sat in on an interview that he had with a journalist from Swaziland.

That was soon after the signing of the Nkomati accord between Apartheid South Africa and Mozambique, and one of the terms of the Accord was that President Samora Machel must expel the ANC, and Mozambique must not be used as a launch pad for attacks on South Africa. After a very length interview about the implications of the Nkomati Accord for the ANC, the Swazi journalist asked O. R. whether the struggle was not a futile exercise in the light of the might of the apartheid regime. The answer that O. R. gave was brief and yet so profound.

It was an answer that once again reinforced the confidence and belief that evil cannot triumph over good. This is O. R.'s response to that question: 'Victory amounts to the sum total of the resolution of problems.' That could not have been an answer given on the spur of the moment. I got the impression that O. R. had pondered deeply about the challenges facing the liberation movement. It is possible that at certain times he may have experienced doubts, but he knew that as a leader, he dare not show weakness or entertain doubt in any way. It must have been during that time of introspection that he found the answer to that question. 'Victory amounts to the sum total of the resolution of problems' was O. R.'s creed and philosophical approach to the solution of problems. Problems were not insurmountable: they could be solved with the correct attitude and approach. That was visionary leadership. That was the kind of thinking that allowed Oliver Tambo to lead the ANC until we came back.

When O. R. gave his report to the 48th National Conference of the ANC on the 2 July 1991 in Durban, he expressed himself in these words:

We did not tear ourselves apart because of lack of progress at times. We were always ready to accept our mistakes and to correct them. Above all we succeeded to foster and defend the unity of the ANC and the unity of our people in general. Even in bleak moments, we were never in doubt regarding the winning of freedom. We have never been in doubt that the people's cause shall triumph.

That again demonstrates his caliber of leadership. Only when he was convinced of the prospects of victory could he inspire others to accept his leadership and follow him – to serve him with loyalty and dedication – based on the firm conviction that 'he had been to the top of the mountain and had seen the promised land'.

The power of Oliver Tambo and the fact that he was the glue who held the ANC together during those difficult years in exile is that he did not see himself as a leader but as a servant of the people. There are various occasions when I felt that O. R. was talking to me not as a leader but more as a father, giving guidance and empowering me, forcing me to think and sharpen my skills of analysis and look at facts and come to correct conclusions.

There are numerous times when we had O. R. as a guest on Radio Freedom and we interviewed him on the position of the ANC regarding the political developments inside the country and globally.

There was never a time when O. R. simply went into the studio and began answering questions. At all times, he would say that 'You guys must have been writing about this issue in your comments; you must have discussed it and taken positions on it; what have you been saying? What conclusions did you come to and why?' We would then spend maybe an hour in intense discussion with him, probing, asking questions and seeking clarification. By the time we conducted the interview, President Tambo would take our views and incorporate them into his own answers and the outcome would be a rich and informed interview with our views and opinions taken into consideration.

I remember many instances where O. R. stands out as the kind of leader you follow voluntarily because you believe that he is leading you where you want to go. He inspires loyalty and trust.

Soon after Nelson Mandela was released from prison, I was informed that President Tambo and Mr Mandela were in transit at Lusaka International Airport on their way to Sweden and other parts of Europe. I drove to the airport in Lusaka and our Comrades working as immigration officers arranged for me to greet President Tambo in the International VIP Departure Lounge. When I entered the VIP Lounge, the two South African Leaders were sitting together having a conversation, and then President

Tambo did an amazing thing: using his walking stick, he stood and greeted me with the words: 'Don (my exile name), it is so good to see you. It has been a long time.' I felt humbled that that great leader of the South African people – that great revolutionary – would stand up for me when I saw myself as a junior person within the ranks of the ANC. And what was further amazing was that President Mandela, whom I did not know personally and whom I was not sure how to approach and greet, also stood up, towering over me, and greeted me exactly as O. R. had done: 'Hello, Don, how are you? You look fine.' It was as if he had known me for all those years.

That, for me, was a moment I would cherish for the rest of my living days. That was the kind of leadership that led the people of South Africa; a leadership that was tried and tested in struggle, and a leadership that considered itself not to be above the people but were servants of the people they led.

Thami Ntenteni

Dear O. R.,

I can't really say when I exactly first met Tata O. R. Tambo, but back then it just seemed like he had always been present in my life. He regularly visited our house at No. 6 Msuzi Road, Woodlands, Lusaka, Zambia.

He wasn't just physically present but emotionally, he always made me feel like anything I had to say or show him was very important to him. I laugh now, because I recall one day, Tata had already been at our home for a couple of minutes, when I had come hopping and skipping into our home from playing in the dusty streets with my neighbourhood friends; and I went directly to him to show him that I just learnt how to do cartwheels!

After I had showed him them, I soon realised that he was not alone and it seemed like there was some deep conversations that had come to a stand still, because little Miss Thandi had was moving across the living room and almost bumping into the furniture doing cartwheels. He would lean back with laughter and say well done!

Like a child then, I played outdoors, so I was always aware when Tata O. R. would be visiting because his security attaché would first drive past our house then a few minutes later Tata's car would arrive with me and my crew running, and waving right

next his car. Of course; it defeated the purpose of him being inconspicuous because by the time he turned into our street and into our yard, I was already screaming at the top of my lungs to my parents that uncle O.R. was about to arrive.

There was one day at our house a lot flurry, I went straight to my mother to enquire what was the matter, and she seemed agitated and hesitant but gave a glance at Tata and he gave her a nod. She subsequently gave me this beautiful white card that had a small cut out at its centre. Through the cut out was a nice picture of Tata's face. To see more, I opened the card and it revealed Tata being neck laced. It saddened me greatly, because I couldn't phantom who would hate him so much!

With him I felt so safe, that nothing could happen to any of us in the ANC; it was indestructible, he and other African leaders had made this happen. So to see him every month made me feel like everything was still A alright; a relief from the uncertainty that was soon to come.

When we had moved into the new South Africa, we were all surprised but yet we were not. Everything that had been done thus far was for this! Tata, always talked about when we move back to South Africa, he always worked for this, he always prepared all of us for this day. It felt like this was a natural progression to now be in a free South Africa!

Tata O.R.'s health had detoriated and the Dr's had done everything possible; it was now for us to keep Tata as comfortable as possible. The last time I saw him was at his home in Johannesburg, South Africa. He was walking in a fragile manner with a walking stick back to his front door from ushering out a visitor. For some reason I froze and to this day I have always regretted that I never went to assist him; I don't know why I just froze!

April 23th 1993, I was visiting my cousin in England, when I heard the passing of Tata. I cried uncontrollably that my aunt had to make me sugary water to prevent me from collapsing. It felt scary; that he who had been the glue that held us together had now left. He who had shielded us from being killed or imprisoned had now vanished. He who had provided education, food, and shelter had descended to another world.

After a thorough introspection, I realised that if Tata was still alive, he wouldn't have been able to do nothing much now; because what he came to do; his task was accomplished; he had completely fulfilled his purpose and that was to bring us back home to a free South Africa!

Rest In Eternal Peace Tata, and thank you!

Thandi Modise

Dear Uncle O. R.,

This year, we are celebrating your life and the legacy that you left with us. I wish that we had celebrated you when you were alive; however, I am honoured and feel privileged to have the opportunity to recognise you.

I was born on 6 January 1972 in Ibadan, Nigeria to my parents Thandi Lujabe-Rankoe and Philip Rankoe. My mother, Thandi Lujabe-Rankoe, worked under your leadership until the time of your passing. My memories of my childhood are of having two extended families who shaped the person that I have become: my nuclear family and the ANC family that was led by you.

While you held the formal role of president of the ANC, I knew you as Uncle O. R. I had the pleasure and privilege of meeting you on several occasions in Nigeria, Zambia, and Norway. I remember you as being warm and gentle and relating well with children. In particular, your smile stands out in my memory. I remember singing songs about you at our Masupatsela sessions:

Uph' uTambo, U Tambo usehlatini bafana
Wenzani na? Ufundisa ama joni
Haihaihaihai 1 line, 2 line bafana ...
Mayibuye, mayibuye iAfrica;
Eyathathwa, eyathathwa nga mabhulu

In Nigeria, one of my earliest memories is of commemorating the death of Solomon Mahlangu by drawing a picture of someone being hanged. Due to the relations you had built in Nigeria with Uncle Thabo and Aunt Zanele Mbeki, my mother and others supporting you, Nigeria was home to numerous South African exiles, in particular, the large numbers of 1976 students who sought refuge after fleeing South Africa. Scholarships, etc. were arranged to ensure their continued education, which was a key pillar for the ANC under your leadership.

We visited Zambia once a year. Zambia was the home of the ANC in exile (at least that was my experience of it). Despite Zambia going through its own trials (I remember the bread queues), the relationship that you had created with the Zambian government meant that the ANC headquarters were established in Zambia, enabling the organisational organs to operate. In addition, the Makeni farm (supported by the Swedish government) for agricultural development.

My mother was the ANC Chief Representative in Norway from 1987–1994. The Norwegians were huge proponents of the liberation struggle of the people of South Africa, and I met you on one of your visits to Norway.

In all of those countries, we were treated with dignity. They were true partners in the struggle for liberation.

One example of the partnership I experienced with the Norwegians was in 1985. That year, there had been a raid on 14 June by the South African Defence Force on the ANC community residing in Botswana. My family were survivors of that raid, after which, my mother was deported from Botswana. The Norwegian ambassador and his family provided me with a home for 6 months so I could finish my school year.

Perhaps I should take the opportunity to say something about the raid. About two days a week, after school, I would spend time at the home of Uncle George and Aunt Lindi Pahle. I was at their home on the day of the raid. My mother came to pick me up later that evening and we went home as usual. Little did we know that that would be the last time we would ever see Uncle George and Aunt Lindi again, as they were murdered later that night.

I woke up the next morning and my mother drove me to school. We lived in Kgale, which is a little way outside of Gaborone. On the way to school, there were roadblocks everywhere and we did not know what was happening. I went to school and remember that one of my cousins, Themba Maqubela, was quite distressed. I

Tsheli Lujabe and mum Lujabe Rankoe

had learnt how to be secretive about my ANC identity for security purposes. When my mother picked me up in the evening and told me about the raid, my heart broke when I heard that Uncle George and Aunt Lindi had been brutally murdered.

So many things changed on that day: I lost my home (we had to move from one house to the next looking for a place to live); I lost my dog, Spotty, who was given to another family and I never saw him again (that was very emotional for me; he was my favourite dog I have ever owned); after the mass funeral for the 12 that were killed, my mother was deported, as she was on the list and, somehow, they didn't make it to our home. I moved into the Norwegian Embassy and left Botswana in December 1985.

What I must say is that I learnt resilience from that experience. I learnt that home is not bricks and mortar: it is where the heart is. I learnt that things can fall apart and you can build them up again and move forward.

Uncle O. R., you, my family and the ANC family really set a great foundation of values that have stood me in good stead throughout my life.

I am a clinical psychologist by profession and had the privilege of achieving that through a number of scholarships I attained over the years of my education. That would not have been possible without the value placed on education in the ANC exile community and the relationships that were developed with numerous donors to support the learning and development of our community in preparation for a free South Africa. I studied clinical psychology in order to work with people who had been affected by trauma and other triggers that lead to mental health challenges. The struggle had a psychological impact on our people, and I wanted to make a difference. I had witnessed how the raids and other atrocities had impacted on our people and I wanted to support them to be resilient and unlock their potential.

What has stayed with me most is the memory of your quiet, inclusive, and selfless leadership. You ensured that the ANC developed relationships with key stakeholders and countries around the world. You ensured that we all lived by the values of respect, hard work, being there for each other, and learning and growth with a vision of freedom. You identified strengths in others and ensured that they developed and could support the cause and vision. You created an ANC in exile that achieved so much through your inclusive leadership – you empowered others, held them accountable, you were courageous and put your personal interests aside for the greater good, and you showed humility in everything that you did.

You did a good job of succession planning, as you ensured that you groomed leaders to whom you could hand the baton.

I currently work in the field of leadership development. There are numerous definitions of effective leaders; however, the one that really resonates with me is the one that states that 'effective leaders lift their followers into their better selves'. I see you as being one of the greatest leaders I have ever known.

Since you left us, sadly, our beautiful country South Africa has been going through numerous challenges. I remain hopeful that there are enough people who have been touched by you and, as a result, we will be able to overcome those challenges and enjoy the freedom that you and others worked so hard for us to realise. You showed us the way and we will try to show others the way.

My hope for the future South Africa:
- Education, education, education ... let us develop a culture of curiosity and learning. Let us unlock the potential of the people of this beautiful country so that everyone can make a contribution to the success of the nation (mediocrity is not an option).
- Let us value our similarities and differences (say NO to tribalism and other 'isms').
- Let us reward and recognise people for their contributions, not who they know.
- Let us ensure that we are transferring skills and building an ongoing pipeline of future leaders in every aspect of society (with everyone being the best that they can be, whether you are a security guard or the CEO of a bank).

Continue to rest in peace, Uncle O. R. May your light continue to shine upon us.

Love,

Tsheli Lujabe (nee Rankoe)

Letter to uTata O. R. Tambo

Dear Uncle O. R.,

Let me begin by wishing you great rest. I was requested by Mrs Pulane Kingston on behalf of Ambassador Lindiwe Mabuza to write a letter in memory of you, uTata O. R. Tambo.

I was born in Leipzig, Germany on 1 April 1971. My first recollection of you was in Lusaka, Zambia at my late grandparent's home at 17 Dombeya Avenue, Lilanda, which was located in Lusaka, Zambia. It was during my late grandfather Duma Nokwe's funeral in 1978 that I first met you. I remember that there was a lot of respectful excitement upon your arrival, and I knew then that a very important man had set foot at home: it was explained to me that you were the President of the African National Congress of South Africa.

I remember your warmth and how soft-spoken you were. I also clearly remember a striking physical feature of yours: markings engraved on both of your cheeks. It was later explained to me that those were '*umgqatshulo wamaMpondo*', and that they signalled great honour within the Mpondo Nation.

I recall that, on many occasions, you would visit my home in Lilanda, in particular, to check on my late grandmother, Mrs Vuyiswa Tiny Nokwe, after the passing of my late grandfather; and you would then walk across the street to visit with the Nkobi family. I would always know that you were within the vicinity, if I saw uTata Nxumalo, one of the uncles that would drive you around. I also recall the late Uncle Mshengu who closely accompanied you everywhere.

The first thing you would always enquire about was how school was going and how well I was progressing at school. That was your primary concern and it demonstrated a deep respect for education, a general trait among the elders in exile. Whenever we think of giants like you, we are grateful that you gave us the lifelong values of hard work, humility and purpose. Your personal example of sacrifice remains forever etched in our memory, challenging us to ask uncomfortable questions of ourselves – questions needing sincere answers about the depth of our commitment to the society you and your comrades sacrificed a lot for. Beyond commitment, we have to determine our purpose and not act uncompromisingly of our convictions. We dare not fail your sacrifice and memory by being and doing the things that are alien to your exemplary existence.

I also recall your love for choral music and cultural dance as you spent time polishing up the choir of the former 'Amandla

Ensemble'. My late mother, Poppy, was a member of the Amandla Ensemble, and she would take me along to their practices in Lusaka, Zambia. I would see you sing along and, at times, conduct the Amandla choir. That part of your personality resonates the most for me as it affirms that, beyond the political sphere, you had a great and genuine spark of humanity in search of love and joy. There were times when, as young ANC Pioneers, certain songs that we performed would be tweaked or changed, and it would be explained to us that those suggested changes came from you. We knew that you always kept an eye out for all of us as the former Masupatsela.

Finally, I would like to mention that, in all of my travels from the former GDR, Zambia, Somafco in Tanzania, and other places where I spent a considerable amount of my life, I always observed that even when there were great challenges and, at times, acute criticisms against the leadership of the ANC, there always remained a deep and genuine respect for you. I believe that that was what managed to keep the ANC united, resolute, focused, and committed to their historical responsibilities during some very tough times in exile. I thank you for that.

During all those years in exile, I have to say, I never went to bed hungry; I had a bed to lie on, and I had access to quality education

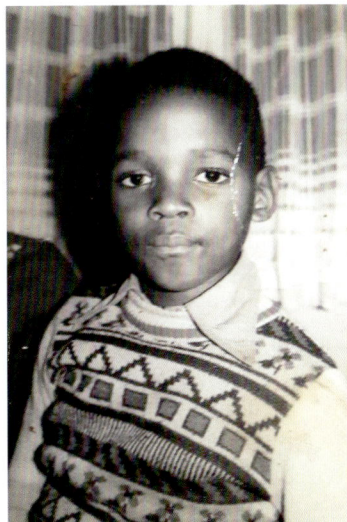

in both Lusaka and Somafco and, later on, at university. Again, I thank you and the great collective that you worked with.

Ndiyabulela, Lala ngoxolo,

Vuyo Pumelele Skweyiya

My recollections of Comrade O. R.

I was struck by his dignity and gentleness ...

It was 1984 at the Solomon Mahlangu Freedom College (Somafco) in Tanzania. We were all excited that the President of the ANC, the man affectionately known as Comrade O. R. had come to visit the ANC School. I was more excited than most because I was due to have a meeting with him. Unfortunately, it was not to be a one-on-one, but I was part of a delegation representing various student bodies. I was the leader of the Pioneers. The Pioneers were a social and political organisation representing children between the ages of 10 and 16 years, and I was going to deliver a status report to our president. All 16 years of me meeting Comrade O. R.!

The meeting took place one sunny afternoon at the house used by our security department in a small suburb named Copenhagen in honour of Denmark and the support it was giving our school. There, we were all seated in the sitting room when in walked Comrade O. R. My first thought, as butterflies played havoc with my stomach, was, 'What a gentle and dignified man.' Here was the friend and Comrade of our president, Nelson Mandela. Here was the man who represented a link between our leaders on Robben Island and the exiled ANC leadership. He was the link that began with the formation of the ANC Youth League in 1949 and the ANC of the present. He was the link between the ANC underground inside the country and in exile. He was the link between the ANC and the international community. Indeed, I will dare add, he was the glue that held the ANC together throughout its most arduous exile years.

We stood up as he entered the room, my heart thumping in my chest. He greeted each one of us individually and, taking my hand in a firm handshake, said, 'Good afternoon, Comrade.' In a hesitant voice, I replied, 'Good afternoon, Comrade President.' 'And what is your name?' he enquired. 'I'm Zola Maseko, and I am here representing the Pioneers,' I replied in a faltering voice. 'The Pioneers? Very good!' He made me feel that I was the most important person in the room. He then sat down and each of us gave him a report about the activities of our various organisations. I told him that the Pioneers had established relations with Pioneers from various other countries. We were also involved in exchange programmes where we sent our members to different countries to tell them about our personal experiences as children of the African National Congress. We shared our experiences of growing up in exile and also learnt a lot about their countries, languages, cultures and struggles. We corresponded with Pioneers from the Socialist Bloc, Scandinavia, Cuba and South America.

That evening, he addressed the entire student body. In his talk, he gave us a summary of the political situation back home. How can I describe Comrade O. R.'s talk to us that evening? I believe it was my fellow student and my late brother Gandhi's best friend, Paradise Mashinini, who articulated it best. He said (and don't ask me how he knew this) that Comrade O. R. was just as powerful as Nelson Mandela. The only difference was that, when Mandela addressed a crowd, you wanted to kill the nearest boer, there and then. Mandela, he said, was an orator who inspired passion and immediate radical action. But after listening to Comrade O. R., you went home and digested his message and then looked for the nearest boer to kill! He ended his talk by telling us to study hard, as a democratic South Africa would need educated cadres to run our economy. After his talk, the students put on a dazzling evening of various cultural performances ranging from gumboot dancing, a short play, poetry recitals and ending with a few songs from the student choir. I vividly remember Comrade O. R. getting onto the stage and conducting the choir! He was passionate about culture and had a particular affinity for the choir. It was a memorable evening.

A few years after that, I joined *uMkhonto We Sizwe*. I was 19 years old and was again amazed at how the very mention of our president's name inspired us! He was, after all, our commander-in–chief, and we sang revolutionary songs. One of my favorite songs was:

UTambo ufuna amajonny, amjonny enkululeko
Tambo needs guerillas, who will fight for freedom

Many years later, I read that, like all of us, he had his own dreams and aspirations before the struggle consumed all of his energies. He had wanted to be a priest. That gentle soul who inspired an army!

As our beloved movement seemingly bobbles towards the abyss, hell-bent on implosion, I often think how different South Africa would be had Comrade O. R. lived to be a part of this new South Africa. Whatever you may say about the ANC, it produced giants, and Comrade O. R. was one of the greatest and stood head and shoulders above his peers, although he would be horrified to hear such a statement!

As for me, what can I say except that I walked with giants ...

Zola Maseko

Dear Uncle O. R.,

I am the first-born daughter of Manto Tshabalala-Msimang, and I came into this world in Russia where my mother was attending medical school. When she completed her medical studies, we moved to Dar es Salaam where she was a registrar in the field of obstetrics and gynaecology.

My first recollection of you was singing freedom songs with your name in them. Most of them were in isiZulu and some in SeSotho. The funny thing is that I could sing the words but had no idea what they meant because, at that time, my understanding of those two languages was virtually non-existent! I pictured you as this 'giant' because I was still very young with a vivid imagination.

My first face-to-face encounter with you was when I was in Lusaka getting ready to go to the then Soviet Union as a Pioneer. Five of us were going (including Silindile Sangweni), and I was flown from Dar es Salaam to Lusaka, from where we were going to leave. We spent time in Lusaka practising dances and songs that we would perform when in Russia. You came to one or two of our rehearsal sessions, and again, it did not register that you were the SAME Uncle O. R. that I had been singing about. You were unassuming and gave us words of encouragement and mostly praise for what we were doing. That gave me a sense of pride, and I hope that I represented us well as a Pioneer in Russia. I do know

that, after that, when I sang songs with your name in them, even though I still may not have fully understood what I was singing about, I sang with more heart because I had met you.

As I grew older, I came to appreciate the enormity of your responsibility, and I came to understand more clearly what you stood for. Your ability to articulate that clearly and at a level that even we young Pioneers could understand, I think helped to shape the young adult I became when I was at university in the United States.

My teenage years were spent living in Dar es Salaam, and I remember my mother would ensure that whenever you were visiting Tanzania, and especially Mazimbu (Somafco), my sister Pulane Kingston and I were there. I distinctly recall a time when my younger sister was reciting a poem (she was fearless) with such heart and passion and you were so moved by her performance. It warmed my heart and endeared me to you – and I think that was the moment that you wormed your way into my heart and mind.

I also remember an instance when you came to where we lived – there were four of us living in a small room that we affectionately called 'Corner B'. It seemed that you had been misled into

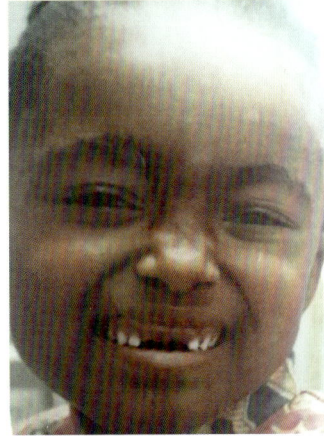

believing that we were living a luxurious lifestyle, and you were appalled to see how we were living. After that, even though we did not necessarily move out of Corner B, at least we were then put on the list and route so that we could receive food like all of the other ANC members living in Tanzania. That was another moment that made me appreciate and respect you immensely.

I have listened to you on Radio Freedom on many occasions and was always impressed by your ability to be so articulate and passionate about your beliefs.

I wish I had been among the many people who welcomed you when you came back to South Africa. Whenever I see footage of that, I smile and have a great sense of joy about that welcome you received. It was with great sadness that I learned that you had passed away (and before that had suffered a stroke), and I truly wish that you would have lived longer and assisted in grooming more principled leaders who would continue the work that you had only begun to do!

The question now is: how have my memories of you shaped who I am today? I would say that they have given me the desire to serve and the desire to work for a South Africa (even now in the midst of all this chaos) where we have access to clean water, basic health services and basic education. I am now part of the Faculty of Health Sciences at the University of Pretoria, where I am the academic coordinator for a new cadre of health care providers – clinical associates – with the view that they will address the continued inequity when it comes to access to quality health care. I have also recently been asked to serve on the Health Science Committee for Transformative Education, which is something that I think I can make an impact in. It remains my belief that we still have a long way to go in South Africa, but I want my children, Msithazwe and Nomkhitha, to be part of a South Africa where they can realise their dreams. I think that being able to vote is only a small step in what is clearly going to be a long journey during which we should continue to fight for improvements. You and others of your generation gave us the tools and the stomach for that – we just need to keep it up!

Remembering you with fondness,

Zukisa Tshabalala

Aw' bheke manje mfowethu, seliyashona
Bamb' isandla sami, seliyang'shiya
Uz' ufik' ekhay' ubatshele la 'ng'shiye khona
Emahlathini aseAngola.
Oliver Tambo bamb' isandla sam'… we Tambo bamb' isandla sam'
Siyolal' emahlathini … sivuke siyibambe …
Usibamb' ungasiyeki ebunzimeni …
Ho thatha nans' ibazooka/stetchkin … shay' ugudlule
Zonke lezinto, zalabaloyi

(Look now my brother, the sun is setting
Hold my hand, it is setting on me
When you get home, tell them where you left me
In the forests of Angola
Oliver Tambo hold my hand … hey Tambo hold my hand
We will spend the night in the bush … then wake up to fight …
Hold it, don't let go in times of difficulty …
Take this bazooka/stetchkin, etc. … hit hard
at all the things of these enemies
https://youtu.be/t-i8z2HUp3Q)

We would hold, shake hands and hug as we sang that song. Turns out it was used by one of our Comrades when he knew that his time to leave for exile had come.

Dear Comrade O. R.,

Thina siphum' eMzantsi neAfrika lapho kubus' ibhunu, Tambo baphel' abantu
Tambo sinik' ibazooka, sinik' iAK …

(We are from the South of Afrika where the white man rules.
Tambo, the people are being decimated
Tambo, give us the bazooka; give us the AK …
https://youtu.be/d2t4-hYjDQs)

As with the struggle for liberation,[1] I met you through song. I had just gotten into my teens and was learning a lot about our history and freedom struggle. Your name inspired courage, self-sacrifice and, as Lungi[2] would say, cast-iron integrity.

---

1. From an early age, music has played a significant role in how the writer experienced life and the struggle.
2. Lungi Kganyago is a childhood friend of the writer.

Uphi uTambo? Utamb' usehlathin' bafana
Wenzani na? Usaqeqesh' amajoni
Fall into line bafana ...

(Where is Tambo? Tambo is in the bush, boys
What is he doing? He is training the soldiers
Fall into line boys ...
https://youtu.be/FvZ7SLmq164)

You became part of our transition from childhood to adulthood: *klip-gooiers* (Afrikaans for stone throwers) to *abothebula* (isiZulu for guerrillas). That transition included the mobile units you had talked about in one of your many speeches. People took pride in subsequently being inducted into the ranks of the organisation and, for some, its military wing *Umkhonto we Sizwe* (Spear of the Nation, also known as MK).

Sasishilo ngo '61,[3] *sath' izinyo ngezinyo ... UTamb' uyabuya ...*

(We had said in 1961, that it's a tooth for a tooth ... Tambo will return ...)

We listened to your voice through the crackle of the short wave Radio Freedom (RF) broadcasts, courtesy of radio stations from Mozambique, Tanzania, Madagascar, etc. Sometimes, we would use RF recordings smuggled into the country. Those were of a better quality and the timbre of your voice would be easier to discern and (for some of us) savour.

Oliver, Oliver e haye e haye thina sixotshiw' ekhaya ... zabalaza ...
Oliver, Oliver molo sotsha ...

(Oliver, oh we are aliens in our land ... hold on to the struggle ...
Oliver, greetings soldier ...
https://youtu.be/8N3Dg-2fmME)

' ... Our task is to make South Africa ungovernable and apartheid unworkable ... Victory lies in the attack ... maintain the strategic initiative ... attack, advance, give the enemy no quarter ...
On behalf of the NEC of the ANC, I declare this The Year of the Women ... the Youth ... the Spear ... the Cadre ... mass action ...' And so it went from one year to the other. O. R., you were very present in our lives.

Sithi ngawo lonyaka womanyano s'khulule Tambo
Ngebazooka, ngemortar neAK ...

(We say during this year of unity, liberate us, Tambo
With the bazooka, the mortar and the AK ...)

---

3. MK was launched on 16 December 1961 through a series of attacks on selected targets.

Then one day, we left the country and Thulani[4] got to meet you. When I subsequently caught up with him, we talked endlessly about that encounter. I can't recall all of the things discussed. Time also mixes up the memories of such conversations with other exchanges. However, some of the things that come to mind are about how you discussed our future plans with him. You had been trying to impress upon him the importance of us pursuing our studies further. He had insisted on the need for us to continue our work and build our units inside the country. That and subsequent encounters brought us closer to some members of the team who worked closely with you. Some of those people left a lasting impression on us.

Amayuyuyu, iyo iyo ...
Mama mamela amaphimbo ezinsizwa ezikaMqabuko ... ezikaOliver
Dlala siyadlala ... giya siyagiya ... songena eMzantsi nges'bhamu, kwelika Oliver

(Singing *amayuyuyu* ... Mom listen to the voices of Mqabuko's[5] ... (and) Oliver's young men
Let us play ... let us dance ... we will enter the South with the gun, in the land of Oliver)

Then there was the issue of your simple lifestyle – as we perceived it. For example, your Lusaka office was said to be fairly modest. I specifically recall how you marvelled at one of the offices abroad. At some point you rode around in a simple white Peugeot and had contemptuously rejected a fancy luxury vehicle (possibly a black stretch limo) that had been offered to you.

Thumelani wemfokaTambo ... lelizwe selizobuy'ekhaya Gatsha khawuyeke lent' ozenzayo ...)

(Send them, son of Tambo ... this country is about to return home Gatsha [and others who were in the service of Apartheid] ... stop what you are doing ...)

By the time I first came into physical contact with you, it felt as if I knew you well. I recall how informal the meeting was. We had finished sports practice and I am sure were reeking with the smell of teenage sweat! You reminisced about the late Basil February,[6] referring to him as a giant. His younger brother or nephew was in our group. I also found it remarkable that you remembered Thulani, despite only having met him once. You presented a fatherly figure. Your hands were very soft. The meeting was held in a Comradely manner. You made us feel like equals. But that did

---

4. Thulani Muthwa (nom de guerre) was in the same outfit as the writer. The former was the commander and the latter, the commissar.
5. Mqabuko was one of the leaders of the Zimbabwe People's Revolutionary Army (ZIPRA). The name seems to be specifically in reference to Joshua Nkomo who later became Zimbabwe's first vice president.
6. Basil February was one of the early MK combatants and contributors to its Journal, the *Dawn*. He led one of the first units as part of the Wankie campaign destined for battle in South Africa via Zimbabwe. He died in action in 1968.

not stop us from basking in the shadow of your wisdom. I think you still tried to raise the issue of studies but were appreciative of our stance at the time. I think you would be proud to know that we have since made some progress on the academic front too.

Sesiyolal' ehlathini, Oliver Tambo
Sivuke ngeAK
Tambo s'khokhele singen' ekhaya ...

(We are going to spend the night in the bush, Oliver Tambo
Then arise with the AK
Tambo lead us, as we enter the home front ...)

Following one of your lectures, we felt vindicated when the people we were staying with told us that they now could see that we were not just talking off the tops of our heads. I remember how you made your entry by running up the stairs leading up to the podium, and then turned around and clasped your hands, greeting those who had gathered for your talk. Years later, I saw Mabel[7] doing a similar sprint up the stairs. She reminded me of you. I think she had worked with you at some point. As usual, you started by greeting the audience on behalf of the movement, the people of South Africa, etc. Then, in what seemed to be

a humorous response to a child who had been crying in the audience, you said: 'I also greet you on behalf of the children.' The hall burst out in laughter!

Iminyak' emashum' amabili ... sesilungiselela umzabalazo
Wayezul' umfo kaTambo ... ezul' ezintabeni, efun' izintelezi zokuphehl' amabutho
Hayi eCuba/Angola ... basifundisa basiqeqesh'a abasebenzi
Siyabonga siyavuya basebenzi
Ningadinwa nangomso!

(20 years of preparing for the struggle
The son of Tambo wondered all over the mountains, looking for herbs to strengthen the regiments
In Cuba/Angola etc. ... the workers taught and trained us
We give thanks to the workers, we are joyful
Don't ever tire!)

There are many other memories ... like the personal spaces shared with those you met and the impact you had on them – including those who took the vow of the spear in your presence. You continue to live through people like them and many others. Lerato[8] once said that you, like our former Chief of Staff[9], tended

---

7. Mabel (nom de guerre) later became a government minister.
8. Lerato (nom de guerre) shared this during a discussion en route to South Africa for her MK work.
9. Chris Hani was MK's commissar and, later, Chief of Staff.

to remember names very well. Both of you had the ability to make people feel special. Cindy[10] once commented on the need for genuine cadres and used you as one of the examples. Zola[11] has exacting standards on herself and others. You remain one of the few faultless men that she has come across.

Tambo s'khokhele mfokaTambo
S'thath' ilizwe lethu
Sombamb' uVoster ePitoli
Simfak' ejele, makahlale khona ngob' akanangqondo ...

(Lead us son of Tambo
As we take our country
We will capture Voster in Pretoria
Then put him in jail where he must stay because he has no brain ...)

Then there is the story of how you practically saved Captain's[12] life. He applied the values that your leadership represented and became an effective and inspiring commander. He once told those who worked with him that he would not allow himself to be captured alive. He was unarmed when he found himself surrounded by the apartheid forces. The story is told of how he charged towards them and fell when a bullet hit his leg. As they tried to pick him up, he started punching until he was overpowered and bundled into a vehicle.

Webaba Tambo thum' abafana hayi hayi hayo
Thum' abafana bazos'khulula
Angola say'thatha njani emlonyen' wes'lwane?
Giji! Hawu!

(Hey father Tambo send the boys ...
Send the boys to liberate us
How did we capture Angola from the mouth of the beast?
Chant ...)

Your presence is still felt in many ways ... especially, through song!

UTambo noSlovo ngamacommando
IFAPLA noMkhonto i alliance ...

(and when we were hungry - *ipapa nenyama i alliance!* ...)
(Tambo and Slovo are commandos
FAPLA [Forças Armadas Populares de Libertação de Angola/ People's Armed Forces for the Liberation of Angola] and Mkhonto [MK] are allies
porridge and meat are allies! ...
https://youtu.be/eJrqAyoR_GA)

Today's lived experience makes some of the things above seem like fiction to others. Questions get asked. Did we know about

---

10. Cindy (nom de guerre) shared this during an encounter in one of the facilities.
11. Zola (nom de guerre) was exposed to underground work at an early age through the work of her father in Swaziland.
12. Captain (nom de guerre) joined MK in the 70s and operated successfully until his incarceration in 1986. During torture, he held out long enough for his units to take precautionary steps thereby saving others from harm.

some of the traits among us? Could we have done more about some of the problems that the movement had back then? When you intervened to stop certain wrongs from happening, did you and your collective do enough about those responsible for the wrongs? How would we explain the changes to the new generation? For example, what do I say to them about a song like the one below that was sung recently by workers:

Le utlwile taba tse monate? Bare Zuma wa tsamaya.
A he, helele mama … ha a tsamaye …

(Did you hear the good news? They say Zuma is going.
Oh yes, mama … let him go …)

Bhambatha Zondi

Some of the songs :
1. 'Tribute to O. R.' by Madosini. Available at https://youtu.be/pyPQ9dXN9ck
2. 'Slovo no Tambo' by Amaqabane. Available at https://youtu.be/eJrqAyoR_GA
3. CWU General Secretary leads 'Sizozabalaza'. Available at https://youtu.be/8N3Dg-2fmME
4. ANC singing 'Bamb' isandla sami'. Available at https://youtu.be/t-i8z2HUp3Q
5. 'Uphi uTambo' by Lerumo La Sechaba. Available at https://youtu.be/FvZ7SLmq164
6. Sasco sings 'Baphel' abantu'. Available at https://youtu.be/d2t4-hYjDQs